What "Back Then" Was Like

What "Back Then" Was Like

and stories passed on by ancestors

Roger C. Elliott

Outskirts Press, Inc.
Denver, Colorado

Outskirts Press, Inc.
http://www.outskirtspress.com

ISBN: 978-1-4327-5012-1

Outskirts Press and the "OP" logo are trademarks belonging to Outskirts Press, Inc.

PRINTED IN THE UNITED STATES OF AMERICA

To my daughters, Alyssa and Lindsey: I offer this as a means of knowing where I came from before you came along. To my wife, Jeanette: I appreciate how you've stood beside me in all endeavors.

I would like to thank my parents: Hollie and Rosie Skaggs Elliott for giving me life and helping me to think rationally.

These stories are dedicated to those who made me aware of them.

A special thanks goes to my sister, Flora, who has always been on my side.

To all my friends and family who are somewhere out there if I need them. I hope you consider this worthy as well.

Table of Contents

Foreword

My brother was about ready to leave home to enlist and then be stationed in Korea. My sister was in high school at Springs Valley, in French Lick, Indiana. Dad was fifty and had been drinking more than he should. Mom on the other hand, was thirty-eight and working every day. At this point in April of 1960, I was expected. Not planned, but expected. So, since Mom had been working in Dr. Spears' home for awhile in Paoli, he became Mom's, and of course, my doctor. He, Mom and the rest of his crew at the Orange County Hospital in Paoli, brought me into this world on the eighteenth of April. I was later told that Dr. Spears looked at my fingers and mentioned that I was going to be an athlete. I was also told that Dad bragged about that. See, apparently something was missing in Dad's life up until then, but after I was born, Dad wrote off drinking "cold turkey." He also quit smoking in 1976, but the damage had been done leaving him with the use of only a partial lung. But, the time between my birth and his death in 1985, he drank only one time that I know of and that was when the Republicans took over county offices leaving his whole crew out of a job.

My childhood was really pretty normal for a kid growing up in the 40's or 50's, but unfortunately I was born in 1960. After Mom's short stint in the hospital, she brought me home to the old house in Abydell and like so many things in life, I didn't know how much Abydell meant to me until it was too late. I guess a part of me will always remain there. Although the house I grew up in was out-dated about 30 years, I loved it better than any house I have ever lived in growing up. But, in 1969, I learned that we would be moving. Mom and my older sister, Flora, who was married and living with her husband, John, in Paoli, found a house in Orleans, Indiana. It would provide us with some things the old house in Abydell couldn't, like indoor water and overall warmth. But, in time I learned that it could never provide me with same the comfort. When I learned that we would move, at first I found it to be romantic. On the other hand, Dad was not in favor of moving. I believe it was because he was not seen as the provider since he was not working full time. But, nevertheless the three of us packed up the old blue '58 Chevy Cheyenne pickup and with the help of Flora and John, we moved to the other end of the county. It was a larger community. It was a good town. It had many advantages. It was the right thing to do. After all, after renting for over 25 years, a family should have the opportunity to buy a house and be able to call it their own. So, this is what Mom did. She and Flora went to the Farmer's Home Administration in Salem and signed the papers. After all these years, she had a home and I applaud her for what she did.

But, after moving away, I spent a great deal of time missing my friends in Abydell, and the French Lick area, and since I was experiencing the "new kid syndrome" in Orleans, I became even more homesick. I had been used to being popular with my classmates at my previous school, and since I acted the same in Orleans as I did in the valley, it took me several years to fit in. See, a new kid cannot act too comfortable too soon. As a newcomer, I needed to be accepted first. But, I was used to leading and this didn't help me fit in initially. In fact, I don't believe I ever felt completely comfortable with being myself in Orleans until I was about a junior or senior in high school. I recall thinking this very thing my senior year when Troy Osborne told me one day while we were in art class, that he thought that I was all right. He said that he really didn't get to know me before--Troy was always the most popular boy in my class and had actually caused me some problems when I moved there by picking at me the way kids do to see how the new kid will react. Apparently, I had never passed the test until my junior year as he saw it. From his comment, I recall thinking "Gee, I have been here since fourth grade!" Maybe up until then I had been trying too hard.

Up to that day in Orleans, all I really had going for me was that I was a pretty good baseball pitcher. But, ever since I could ever remember, all I ever wanted to do was play professional baseball. Shoot, that was not my goal. A goal is something that a person shoots for and might not make it. I can't ever remember really planning anything else when I was young. In fact, this was a problem when the career fair time rolled around. See, I was supposed to choose a career and then research it and finally set up a program where parents could come in and see our presentations. Well, being new to the school, I was too embarrassed to say that I planned to choose baseball as a career. That was too ambitious for a new kid. After all, I already knew that players did not choose to play professionally; the professional teams chose them. I couldn't tell anyone, but I just knew I was going to make it. It seemed so realistic. I could virtually see myself playing in the majors. Plus, I don't think that my teacher would have allowed me to choose professional baseball. It was just not a good plan of action for a youngster. So, I settled in with Philip Daughterty who knew what he wanted to do. He wanted to be a gunsmith. I really didn't know anything about "smithing," but I needed a grade. It's too bad grades cause us so much concern. I see now that this was actually cheating. I had to lie for fear that I may be mocked for planning to play baseball my entire life. It may have been different if I had stayed back in Abydell; nobody would have mocked me. Everybody knew me and above all accepted me.

Then, later on when we needed to spend a full day with a person who was a specialist in that area, there were no gunsmiths, so I chose to become a teacher. Although I had lied, God knew what I should do.

I guess it just wasn't in the cards for me to play professional baseball even though I actually got pretty close to being signed a couple of times. I can say now that I just was not talented enough. I did become a teacher after my baseball career looked dim. But, if it were not for baseball, I might not have become a teacher. See, since I couldn't quite make it as a baseball player, I wanted to help others make it instead. So, I wanted to coach baseball and the quickest way to do this was to first get a teaching job on the high school level. Well, I got my first teaching job because I was supposed to be a good coaching prospect. In fact, I was probably one of the youngest head coaches in the state of Indiana when I started. Just two years after graduating from college, I became a varsity coach at Springs Valley High School--where I would have gone to high school if we had not moved to Orleans in '69. But this job did not allow me to coach and teach; there was no teaching job available. So, this is when I applied for my current teaching job at Northeast Dubois High School. I truly got the teaching job in 1987 because I wanted to coach baseball. I had played the game many years, but I had very little coaching experience. It seemed that I was very well accepted when I began, but after the first year I didn't produce a winning team, the locals turned on me. I didn't give in. Although I worked as hard as I could, I couldn't provide them with pitching arms. So, I coached baseball there for nine years, not very successfully I might add, although I believe we had very competitive teams the last three years I coached.

Immediately afterwards, I moved on to coach a newly formed (Single A) independent, professional team. I really loved this job and for the first time I felt appreciated for what I could do. However, this professional job didn't pay me well enough to quit teaching, so after a couple of years coaching the Dragons, I realized that I should stay with teaching. This is when I left the team; I say this because I chose not to reapply the next season after Manager RC Lichtenstein was let go. So, I continued teaching at NE Dubois while I went back to school to get my Masters Degree. I was thankful to baseball because it got me here, but I guess I was just a pretty good sized fish in a small pond as a player. Even though I couldn't play as well as I initially intended when I first started playing ball in the yard in Abydell and later on in high school in Orleans, the game got me where I am today.

When I was 24, after working out with the Louisville Redbirds, the Triple A team for the St. Louis Cardinals, my cousin, David, who lived near Louisville, and was there watching, asked me why I didn't stay on with the team. He actually said, "You looked like you really didn't try out there." But actually, I did try and he couldn't really tell because I didn't stick out as a great player. Apparently he had high expectations. He thought I would walk right in and really impress the world. But, I was just average. Afterwards, Jim Fregosi, who worked me out, asked me for my age and my phone number. Later, one of his assistants told me that I had "a nice arm" and asked my age. I told him that I was twenty-four and he replied, "That's too bad, you should already be here." I understood that he meant if I had been seen earlier and had a chance to go through the whole system, I may have had a chance, but since I was already twenty-four and had not gone through their farm system, it would be pretty hard for me to make it. See, I would have been too old after several years in their minor league system. I never heard from him after that day. But, what most people do not realize is this: To be a professional ball player in any sport, a player has to be good most of the time. I know that even when I was playing well, I was just not good enough, often enough. I had the work ethic for three years in college. Two years were spent at Vincennes Junior College—probably the best team I ever played on was my sophomore year when we went to the region tournament. But after a pretty good partial junior year at the University of Evansville, I had lost my drive to better myself as a baseball player and the injuries started to pile up. Coach Brownlee, my coach at the University of Evansville, told us one day that after many years coaching he could always tell when a player was losing interest. He went on to say how the player would start leaving his glove in the dugout after games or practice sessions. I'll have to admit that he was right because there were several days by the end of my junior year that I couldn't find my glove. I eventually found it the next day in the ball cart where someone had taken care of me the day before. But, back home Dad was 73 years old and going down hill every day, it seemed. Every day down there I worried about losing him.

Although baseball wasn't going as well as I had wished my junior year, fortunately I had just fallen in love with Jeanette Marie Renn. I couldn't imagine leaving her if I continued to play. And again, there wasn't a day that I'd rise that Dad's poor health didn't have an effect on my preparation and play. He lasted until I graduated from from Evansville, but didn't live long enough to see my wedding. On the other hand, I think he lost his will to live when it didn't look like I was going to play professionally--a part of me died too when I discovered that I just couldn't make it as a player. I'm so glad that I had Jeanette and a college education to fall back on afterwards.

On the other hand, I thank my God and my family for experiences that led me to want to play baseball. Baseball allowed me to get the athletic scholarship and to eventually get my college diploma. That college diploma allowed me to get my teaching job. The teaching job, besides providing for my family's needs and keeping me positive about the world I live in, has led me to teach and study writing.

The Bible tells us that God knew each and every one of us even before we were conceived. Well, I believe as I tell my story that God was with me even before I was born. He moved my family from Kentucky to Indiana. He brought me into a world that was unique for most people my age. Unique because most kids growing up in the 60's never had to experience the living conditions into which I was born. Although life was tough, I still consider myself truly privileged and I wouldn't trade these experiences. They have given me a truly unique perspective for life.

1

Back to a Simpler Time

Looking down at the granite gravestone inscription I can't help but recall Granddad's words back in 1980. "Check on the tombstone from time-to-time and see that it isn't knocked over. . . kids do that kind of stuff and I dreamed last night that 'Minnie's' [actually Menta's] stone had been knocked down," he said with a sad face and a glimpse of a tear in his eye. And it wouldn't be long before he would be lying right there beside her on the side of the hill in Crystal. In fact, it was May 1981 to be exact. Now, because of a job that had moved Jeanette and I to Dubois, Indiana, in 1988, I live only three miles from Crystal Cemetery—my grandparents' final resting place. My uncle, Woody Freeman, was also buried in Crystal and recently I, too, made arrangements for my family to be buried there.

I guess it took some time for me to wonder about what my grandparents had gone through before I was born. While Granddad Harve was alive I wasn't at all interested, or maybe I didn't know enough to ask about why his family up and left Sandy Hook, Kentucky, back in the 1950's. But now I wanted to know. I had heard stories about how Uncle Jack, after he had done his tour in the Army, spent his last dollars to purchase a farm in Kentucky. But, Dad and Granddad apparently had had enough since they left and set out for Indiana, regardless. Uncle Jack was said to have lost money on this deal. He had bought a farm for the whole family to work in hopes of making life better for the Elliotts. Little did I know at the time when I had heard about this that Granddad and Mammaw had just too many bad memories to continue living in Kentucky. I didn't know this until I was forty-seven years old.

One day in the summer of 2006 I was talking with my sister and asked her if she knew of any Elliotts back in Elliott County, Kentucky. She said, "Oh, yes, there is Burns and his family still there and I think another of Will's boys may be still around there. And Mom's family has some people scattered around the area. They lived there close when they were kids. Mom and Dad knew each other a long time before they got married because they all grew up together." Why didn't I know this, I thought. Why did I not know anything about my family's life before me. After all, my older brother and sister had both been born in Elliott County. I was the only Hoosier-born Elliott in my family. Some of my other cousins were born in Indiana, but not one had the Elliott surname. So, I talked to Jeanette and my daughters and asked my sister Flora and her husband to go with us and visit Sandy Hook. I told her that I just wanted to see what it was like down there. I said that there was something that I just had to find out. I really didn't know what I was looking for or even why this meant so much to me right now. I guess it bothered me to know that I had a baby brother buried there that I didn't have the opportunity to know because he was still-born before my family moved to Indiana. Jeanette, was wonderful about my curiosity--she has always been supportive in any matter I felt strongly about. So, we made plans and found a lodge on the outskirts of the small town. The lodge was called Laurel Gorge and we took off on a Friday night about 5:00. We arrived in about five hours and checked into the lodge. I somehow felt comforted that I had made the trip and looked forward to the next day's visiting. We made plans to stop in and meet Burns and his family. I, of course, didn't know them and they didn't even know I existed, since I was born in 1960. All they recalled was my brother, Harvey and sister, Flora Mae. Of course they knew Mom and Dad and Granddad Harve and Mammaw "Mint," as Flohrene (Burns's wife) called her. Flohrene said Mammaw always reminded her of Burns' mother, Alice. Well, Burns was Dad's cousin— our grandfathers were brothers. And Burns was living close to his daughter, Dianna and her family. There was family in and out of their doors all day and I didn't know any of them. Unfortunately though, it wasn't long after being there that I learned Burns was in bad shape and had cancer in his spine. I couldn't tell this if Dianna hadn't mentioned it except for the fact that he never got up out of his recliner. In fact, he never complained while I was there. I truly believe he enjoyed our visit. I hope our visit allowed him to somehow forget his anguish for a little while. He was probably the nicest man I had ever met. In fact, I asked my sister why I had not heard of him. Well, Burns heard me and replied jokingly, "'Why didn't you tell him about me?'" He and his family were only a half-day's travel away and--I wish I had visited years before. I kept wondering why I hadn't acquired the interest to ask about him when I was younger.

Although Burns wasn't well, he spent time with me telling of how when he was younger he'd visit my Mom and Dad. He said he'd visit them when they were first married. This must have been in 1937 or '38. He also told me about how crazy my dad was "about a ball game" and how one day Mom "nearly gave him a whippin'." After a good laugh, I asked him if he remembered where my grandparents lived. "If you go right across KY 32 there [and pointed] and down Howard's Creek a little piece, you'll be right where your family lived," he replied. Right then something caused me to come alive. I didn't know that I was so interested in this sort of thing. Apparently, they had lived there and other places trying to make a living years ago. Listening to his stories I could just imagine their faces in this setting. It was as if they were here again with us.

Dianna listened to her father give us directions and because he could not go, she loaded us up in her Dodge mini-van and tried to show us what he meant. Just being in the same area made me feel Dad's presence. He had passed away in 1985 and I had missed him every day thereafter. After returning home from this wonderful visit to Sandy Hook, I got a very sad phone call telling me that Burns had passed away. So, now I'd lost another Elliott that could have, in time, been a close friend. I didn't know him really well, but the time we spent together was what I'd needed and I found myself missing him like I'd known him for years, not days. Although I only met him twice, I will never forget how from his information, I finally learned that many generations of Elliotts lived just a few miles away in Precinct One of Sandy Hook.

The Internet became my source of research now; I had learned enough from Burns to want to know more. And, what I found out from death certificates and old census records made me dig for truths. Why had my family moved away from their homeland? They were Elliotts and they lived in Elliott County. This seemed to be where they were supposed to stay. Why didn't they remain there?

Back at Crystal Cemetery, as I was cleaning off old decorations from my family's graves and basically watching over them like Granddad asked, I started wondering about the facts I had heard pertaining to how many kids they had had. Dad always told me he was the oldest of thirteen, but somehow I couldn't recall thirteen aunts and uncles combined. Oh how I wish I would have been more inquisitive about my heritage. "But, what can I do now?" I wondered. Then all of the sudden I got an idea. "Thank goodness, Aunt Lucy is still around," I thought. And I took out for Muncie, Indiana, where she had lived for many years. I learned from her that she was the first to move to Indiana and then the rest of the family came along soon afterwards. I also learned from her that she and my dad had several brothers and sisters, besides the ones I had known, that died in Kentucky. In fact, at least four died before moving to Indiana. To this day, I haven't figured out who the thirteenth child was that died, but I believe it was a baby named Dollie. I haven't found a death certificate to prove that point, but I believe Lucy told me about two sets of twins that died in the "Blue Grass State." However, I did find three that had died, specifically one stillborn, and two under the age of one. But, I haven't found if I heard Lucy right or not, but I do believe she mentioned a Dollie and I know I had heard that name from Dad. Unfortunately again, I can't find out anything more from Lucy either; she died (as did a part of me) spring (2007). Although she is gone now, I recall visiting her because every time I called out to her before walking into her home from the back door, I'd always call out,

"Aunt Lucy, it's Roger, can I come on in?

"'Yeah, if your nose is clean,'" was always her response.

Her daughter Linda "Susie" and I keep in touch still and I treasure her friendship. Just a few weeks ago (the summer of 2009) Linda and

Aunt Elaine's son, Donny and his girlfriend and the girlfriend's daughter spent the night with us in Dubois. Just before retiring for the evening, she read this manuscript and encouraged me to have it published because there are a lot of people out there who need to think back at the good relationships they once had like I have tried to capture here. She commented that people don't take the time to know about the past and about how she cherished the times she had visiting my parents when they lived in Abydell. We also talked of course, about her mother, my Aunt Lucy and told how difficult it was for her to take care of her mother weeks before she passed on. She said it seemed that Lucy didn't have much patience with her because she was so sick. In fact, she often had little spats with her mother because of both of their situations, which is absolutely the same as I have experienced dealing with my mom now. But, my favorite story she told was about how Aunt Lucy would pray out loud in bed. Specifically, one time she heard her talking. She knew nobody was there for Lucy to talk to, so it kinda scared her I guess. So, Linda decided to ask,

"'Mom, who are you talking to?"

"'I'm talkin' to the Lord if you don't mind!'"
Aunt Lucy called back with a tone of discord.

I don't really know why Lucy seemed to love me so much more than any of my other aunts, but she did. I know she did. I suppose she was close to me because she always followed my baseball career and even traveled with Woody to Lakeland and St. Petersburg, Florida to watch me play. They enjoyed baseball, and the Cincinnati Reds—Woody died in 1982 of a heart attack after traveling back from a Reds game. Being at college, I am sorry to say that I was not able to get to Woody's funeral. It hurts me now to think that I wasn't able to go.

After more researching, I found that Granddad and Mammaw lost three children in a year's time! One, the stillborn son named Carlie, his brother Harlie, who died after a couple of months, and then in the same year (nine months later) they lost Mollie Mable who was born in September 1912 (died in November 1913). I presume she was the one I had heard about who had drowned in a flood. I recall hearing from Dad that a sister had been swept away after a hard rain swelled the surrounding creeks of Sandy Hook. Although the baby was never found, I somehow recall although that Dad found some hair that appeared to be hers clinging to some brush and sticks in a nearby branch. So, if this wasn't enough hardship, years after these disheartening circumstances, there was another son, a teenager named Steven Taise Elliott, (born January 16, 1920) who everyone called "Bud." He was apparently found dead in a field after he had been missing for a day and night. I recall Dad telling me that when he found his body, it was frozen to the ground. "Bud's" death really puzzles me because I haven't found anything certain about how he died or even the exact year. Nor have I found a death certificate. But, I had heard many times about how they brought his body back home and kept it in the shed for his Wake. Mom said she recalled that she was pregnant (with Billie, I would guess) and wasn't permitted to "see" him because in those days it was thought that if an expecting mother saw a dead person while pregnant, her own baby would die. Well this didn't stop Mom. She said she slipped out of the house anyway when the others were out working in the fields and visited Bud's lifeless body. She says to this day that she "'just had to.'" It is evident that she loved him so much she couldn't stand not seeing him just one last time. Recently she added that she had just made him his favorite pie. Nearly seventy years later, her face still appeared sad as she commented that "'he never got a bite of it.'" This must have been in 1938 he died, because she said the baby she was carrying died in 1938 too.

After finding all of this, I was beginning to find a whole new respect for my family members. My grandparents' losing three children in a year's time and then another as a teenager and remember, I still haven't found what happened to Dollie. Plus, to this day, 69 years after Bud's death, nobody seems to know who killed him. I even remember asking Burns about this and he sure enough recalled it, but didn't know who killed Bud. He said no one was charged with the murder probably because there was very little police force back then. Why didn't anyone know about this? Why were there no records to be found? Didn't anyone care? Nobody seemed to look into the matter, I guess. But someone told me that Bud had been beaten by a cousin once before and that same cousin refused to pay respects to him while he lay dead in Granddad's shed, before he was buried in Atkins Cemetery on KY 7. In fact, on a later visit in the summer of 2008, a distant-cousin, Earl Elliott introduced me to a man who he said remembered my parents. He seemed very interested and friendly talking about my parents. But, after a few minutes of friendly conversation, I just had to ask if he recalled my Uncle Bud. He immediately recalled Bud's death. In fact he offered that his brother was with him when he was killed.

"So, what happened? What killed him? Do you know?"

"I don't know. . .nobody ever talked about it. I don't know."

He became increasingly quiet from then on. I knew at that moment, that I was not going to hear anything more whether he knew or not. I don't at all suspect that he knows. If he did he probably wouldn't have mentioned that he knew anything about it. So, nevertheless, I made Bud a marker and placed it in the graveyard afterwards, although I really didn't know exactly where he was buried. At least he now has a marker that states he died in 1938.

My daughter, Alyssa and I walked up the side of mountain to the pitifully maintained burial ground and then placed a white cross inside a hollowed out tree near the spot Bud had been laid to rest. This was apparently the only visitation the grave site had probably gotten over the last 25 years except for the cattle that found the shady area a refuge from the hot Eastern Kentucky sun.

Then, there's the grave of my brother, Billie. Although Mom told me that the baby was born dead and was buried in the same grave with a baby cousin who had died on the same day, I haven't been able to find who the cousin was. All Mom recalls is that it was one of Dad's cousins who also experienced a still-born baby on the same day and to save space and money, they were buried together. Nobody has been found yet who knows for sure of the location either, but we suspect that he was buried in the Weddington Cemetery on the corner of Ky 7 and Neal Howard's Creek. So with this, my daughters, Alyssa and Lindsey, and my wife, Jeanette, and her parents, along with the assistance of my aging mother, placed a marker in that grave yard inscribing: "Believed to be the

infant son of Hollie and Rosie Elliott. 1938."
It is truly a shame that there aren't records that
prove where he was laid to rest, but my family could not afford a monument for him nor
my father's brothers and sisters who passed
away when the Elliotts lived in Elliott County.
However, because of the ways the family
members had been buried helped me understand that the Elliotts had a rough time down
there. Before doing this research, I couldn't
begin to understand how hard the times were
back then and why my family moved on. I do
know that my dad loved Kentucky and often
discussed how aesthetically beautiful it was in
Eastern Kentucky. Apparently there were too
many bad memories and not enough money to
stay.

2

The Skaggs Family

It has been two years now that I have also been trying to find where Loella Skaggs, my mom's mother, was laid to rest. She died when Mom was relatively young. That would have been 1935. All I had heard was that she was living in Elliott County at the time of her death and she was buried in Lawrence County (Blaine) in a family cemetery alongside her son by a previous marriage, Leonard Smith. Later, I found that Mom had been a little confused about the burial site, or should I say the county of the site. I, of course had never met Grandma Skaggs and this makes me even more interested in where she was buried. I had planned for some time now to send for her death certificate and if it cannot be found, I planned to at least look up Leonard's death information to see if it mentioned where he was buried. Probably the reason for all of this confusion as to where family members were interned had to do with the Elliott County's Courthouse having burned around 1958. In fact, I still recall what a difficult time Dad had getting a copy of his own birth certificate when he was about to retire. Many have told me that nearly all documents were destroyed or could not be found and this fact is authenticated by many of the Internet websites. Although there are many surrounding counties that have pretty good information about births, deaths, and family history; Elliott County has not been able to catch up. Nevertheless, I thought, there must be some answers somewhere and I just had to keep plugging away. See, I have a bit of competitiveness in me; my wife, Jeanette doesn't refer to this quality necessarily as a virtue. Somehow I can recall her mentioning the words "obsessive-compulsive." I have never agreed to that tag, but I am a person who wants things now and I usually will work diligently day and night until I get what I want. So, with the assistance of Flohrene Elliott, in Sandy Hook, and her long-time family friend, Laura Rachel Farley, I kept going. Actually, I didn't know that I would have anything in common with Ms. Farley, but I made the call and since Flohrene called her and explained who I was and what I was inquiring, she agreed to meet with me at her beautiful home. She has been a God-send to my research. To be specific, I learned that Ms. Farley is now a retired schoolteacher who recollects both sides of my family and even where they lived. In fact, when I asked about Harve Elliott's family, she said very calmly, "Yes I remember all of them." Then she continued to mention specifically my aunts and uncles by name——on both the Elliott side and the Skaggs' side! And when I requested to know about where they lived, she immediately turned to her right and commented, "well, it was right over there." She pointed to the hollow approximately 400 yards adjacent to her back yard. She also said that her sister, who is now somewhat hearing impaired, still recalls my dad visiting her nearly daily. So, in 2008, because I was so elated to find out this much and wanted so much to be able to share this with Mom, I called Mom to tell her that I was right in the same neighborhood where she and Dad grew up. She had a great memory, but she could not show me exact places because they just didn't look the same. While on the phone with her, I told Mom that I had met Laura Rachel Farley and Ms. Farley had explained that although she was pretty young at the time, she still knew that the Elliotts and the Skaggs lived very close and "they often played right there in our yard with my older sisters." Laura Rachel also showed me where the post office was once located, which was run by her family and that this area was the "meeting place" for all the kids in the area. I felt I had hit the jackpot! In fact, the very next weekend my sister, my mom and I made another jaunt back to their (as Dad often said) "old stompin' grounds." When we got back to Sandy Hook with Mom, we checked in at the Inn and then got back into the car and drove around. I showed her this and that and actually wasn't planning on actually visiting anyone yet, but when I drove by Laura Rachel's sister's house, I just had to stop because I saw Mildred sitting on the front porch alone. Something told me that I just had to stop right then and there and I'm glad I did. When their eyes met, Mildred said out loud "Rosie Skaggs." I could tell that she just couldn't believe that she was seeing Mom. In fact, she told me earlier that she just couldn't place my Mom. But, it didn't take her long to recognize her when she saw her in person. They had a wonderful visit and I enjoyed it as much as they did. Then, I just had to use my cellular phone to call next door and when Mom hobbled out of the car at Laura Rachel's home, Mom made her way to her and immediately they hugged. They were not as consistent with their recollections as we had experienced with Mildred, but they had a great visit. While they were talking though, Mom experienced a flashback and commented, "I remember being scared to death somewhere around here because there was some place that had geese that chased me when I was little." And Laura Rachel said, "We had the geese!"

This time we were able to find a great deal more about my family's experiences in Sandy Hook. Interestingly, we found that just beside Laura Rachel Farley's home was the location of the Walnut Grove School. The school is gone now, but it made us very happy to be able to show Mom where she and Dad and the Farley's once attended the one-room schoolhouse. Mom replied, "I remember now. I loved my teacher, Miss Redwine." I remember tearing up when her 86- year-old, timeworn, memory kicked in. Flora and I felt so happy to share this moment with her. Although sharing the moment at Walnut Grove was a wonderful experience, we were not done yet. As I said earlier, it had been over two years that I had been looking for my grandmother Skagg's burial site. After hours and hours of searching physically and on the Internet, I finally found a cemetery in Morgan County, Kentucky, that held the body of my grandma since her death when Mom was only thirteen. She was laid to rest in Fannin Cemetery, on Route 172, near Crockett, KY in 1935. The cemetery had been established in 1880. Mom had told us for years that "Mommy is buried right beside the spot we buried Leonard." Leonard was her brother, who had died a couple of years after Grandma Ella Skaggs in 1937. When we found the cemetery, Mom immediately broke down crying and speaking to the graves of her mother and Leonard stating that "maybe we will be together soon." This may have been the single nicest gift we could have ever given her, Flora told me. Now, for anyone who in the future may want to visit this site, there is one note I'd like to make. The spelling of Skaggs is incorrect on the stone since it is spelled Scaggs. This was probably another reason it was so difficult to find.

3

A Treasure Recalled

Although I'd write this first sentence many times since I initially wrote it, many of the same memories would still rush past me time and time again. Each time they'd be so thick that I could easily have swished them away with my hand. But, I would never want to because while reminiscing, I'd find peace from all those experiences.

Of all those times, I'd particularly remember one pleasant day, down in the bottom. The bottom was located just below where Dad would lay night after night in his hammock listening to any baseball game his old brown transistor radio would get until it was time for him to come in to bed. The bottom was also where my whiffle ball field would (a couple years later) be laid out from scratch. When she approached me, I hadn't thought about whiffle ball yet, but this part of the lower yard would soon be very important to me. The ball field itself would become, as much as I could construe at my young age, a real stadium. Little would I know that what was about to happen when a neighbor's mom called out my name, would be the beginning of my most treasured memories. Before I met my friends, I had not even considered a whiffle ball park, but in my mind a couple of years later as we'd play there. It would be to me a real stadium——just like the Mets' stadium in New York's borough of Queens. My friend, Barry and I still refer to it as Whiffle Ball Stadium. It would be my yard's version of Shea Stadium of course, because the real Shea may as well have been a million miles away from Abydell, Indiana. The only way I figured I'd ever see it was on the old black and white Admiral television located in the front room of our house. See, I had heard of the Mets from television and from my dad--he actually placed a round Mets insignia on our front door glass showing his affiliation as a part-time scout. He had received it from a scout he had somehow met along his way. And when they'd win the pennant and World Series in '69, they would be my team from there on. Plus, Dad was a baseball man. Nobody could doubt that. He was the most interested man I had ever met when it concerned baseball. He said he was a Pittsburgh Pirates fan exclusively, but in reality loved all major league teams. He loved baseball. He'd been a semi-pro player in his day, and afterwards he'd somehow been a "bird dog" scout for the Mets. --Never got famous, never made any money at it, never really cared. But, somehow I had acquired his love for the game and I suppose that would be why I am writing about how I got the idea for making the field.

On this day, she came walking out of the tunnel and stopped as soon as she knew I saw her as if she didn't intend to walk any farther than she had to. The tunnel was a dark, cavernous dwelling underneath the old Monon railroad. This place was located about seventy yards from our front porch, right in our front yard. It was dank and large enough to drive a

Volkswagen "Bug" through, although nobody in his right mind would try to do so. It had been a thoroughfare for my family since we would cut through the tunnel when the water level wasn't up. See, when it rained hard, the branch that ran from the spring up on the back side of Wilson's hill'd swell and pour its contents into the tunnel on its way to the nearby creek. But on this day the water level was down and the tunnel was completely dry. So a neighbor lady easily found her way through the tunnel and to the top step where she could see me playing around in the bottom.

"Roger," she yelled.

Without a call back to her, I walked in her direction. I was surprised to see her. I couldn't ever remember any of our neighbors coming to our house by way of the tunnel. The tunnel was off–limits to me because of the possibility of snakes or whatever. Anyway, I had always been told to stay out of there. So I played there every chance I could. She had walked down the county road past the only stop sign in the village and continued until she left the road to join up with the walking path that entered the tunnel. The whole trip was not more than a couple of football fields long. I recognized her as Mary Hamilton, or at the time, Mary Maul. She had been remarried. I had heard Hamilton as her last name more than I'd heard Maul because my older brother and sister had played with her boys: Tuffy, Frosty, and Rex, and her girls: Janice and Marilyn, when they were all kids in Abydell. Both her family and mine had second generation children. Hers of course, was from a second marriage, but Mom and Dad had me for another reason and I don't think it was purposefully. But anyhow, I knew it was her.

"Joey goes to church at Ames Chapel and Wednesdays they have kid's church activities and he was wondering if you would like to go with him this week. Ask Rosie and Hollie if you can go as Joey's guest . . . if you'd like ta go," she said as she stood there at the entrance of the tunnel.

"I guess I'd like to," I said nervously, not really knowing what I was getting myself into.

"Then you ask yurr mom."

"I will. Do you want to talk to her? She's on the back porch cannin' or somethin'."

"You can tell her," Mary said.

I didn't even wonder why she wouldn't go

on up to the house after she had come this close. I was more interested in the fact that I apparently had a neighbor about my age that wished to invite me to do something. I was engulfed with two feelings. I was excited about the unknown and curiously insecure about doing something without my parents. It wasn't so much that I would have to go to church that bothered me—I didn't go often, I was really thinking about what it would be like to spend the evening with someone I really didn't know, without Mom or Dad. But on the other hand, I really wanted to meet her son, Joey.

A few hours later Mary would give Joey permission to come to my house to talk to me about Wednesday. He too would show up near the tunnel. Later on I'd learn that he was the type of kid that'd always let his mother do the talking for him. But this time, after she broke the ice for us, he appeared. I guess she figured that I might go if I knew him a little. Apparently they were having a contest to see who could get the most kids to show up as guests.

"Hey. I'm Joey. I live over there."

He pointed toward the electrical sub station, the center of Abydell, near the Y. I knew of his house. It stood really close the road that runs out to the highway.

"Would'ya like to go to Ames Chapel Church Wednesday night?" he asked.

"Maybe. I don't know; I haven't talked to Mom or Dad yet," I responded. Since his mother had left, I had been too busy playing in the branch setting up a dam for the next time it would rain. But I knew that it was the church that my sister used to go to before she was married and moved out.

"How old are you? I'm six now," said Joey.

"I'm six too," I said.

"How come you're not in school?"

"I'm goin' this year to first grade," I exclaimed.

"I was in first grade last year, Mom sent me early," exclaimed Joey.

"Wow, this kid's my age," I thought, "and he seemed nice." It seemed weird because I'd heard that I should not go to their house because his mom, Mary, would run me off if I did something wrong. I'd heard from my dad that she was strict and I don't have any business over there. I guess they were protecting me like when they said I shouldn't play in the tunnel.

Mary seemed really nice. And like the tunnel, I liked her now. Maybe she had had a bad day once when my sister or brother was over at the Hamilton's house and things got a little out-of-hand. But all I could go by now was that a nice neighbor lady had asked me to church and that seemed really neighborly--I liked her.

"You better stay out of there; George and Myrtle are in there and they might get you," Dad would say. I even had heard my sister mention that George and Myrtle lived in the tunnel. But she always said this and half-way smiled. Her smile had always made me feel safe. Kinda like she would always be there for me. And to this day, I'm 49, she has been. But I was afraid of that tunnel. And I wasn't going down in that tunnel, at least until nobody was around to see me go. I don't know why, but I was afraid of that tunnel when they told me about it. However, when I was alone, my curiosity was stronger than any fear I had. So I liked to go to the tunnel and look around even though I was afraid of what they told me. In fact, I remember I went there (always alone) and looked to the right and left before entering. There were always vines on the right so thick that I couldn't possibly walk through them and the incline on the left was high and steep. But on the left, there was a huge rock and I'd figured that George and Myrtle lived under this part. I still recall climbing around this cliff and walking up towards the railroad. But when I went down into the tunnel, there were about three natural steps strategically placed to walk down. When Dad and I'd walk up the railroad to get our Christmas trees, or hunt mushrooms, we'd climb up this left side. I recall always wondering how this walking path came to be made. Later, I had it in my mind from all the stories I'd heard over the years, that it must have been left over from where the train man got off to bring the mail up to our house a hundred or more years ago. Legend had it that our house used to be the post office for the community. I also concluded that maybe it was where the silhouettes got off the train when they visited the house at night--I had envisioned this when I was nearly asleep every time a train passed. But there were times when I had personally mustered up enough courage to enter the tunnel. If it had rained hard in a short amount of time, I'd have to walk through the water. It actually flowed all the way over the steps. And when I walked through it, I recall having to step from rock to rock so not to get my shoes too wet. It was a really neat place. I never was hurt in the tunnel and nobody ever got me like Mom or Dad said. But now that I'm older and still think about the tunnel from time to time, I know they were just protecting me since the tunnel couldn't have been too safe for a kid to play. Nevertheless, I would stare at the tunnel from our porch when it was too rainy to go out in the yard. I would keep a good lookout for signs of George and Myrtle, but usually from a safe distance. Remember, it was from under a rock located just to the left side of the tunnel entrance that I expected them to appear. Next to the path the area under the rock was dark and the rock was big—-there's no wonder what could be under there! So I didn't like it much, but I loved it a lot more. Anytime that I just had to go through there, I hurried. But I liked the fear. It was real fear. The type of fear that made me need to go near it even though the hair on the back of my neck would become very sensitive to the air.

Well, Mom said that she would like for me

to go to church at Ames and that it would be nice if I'd go on Sundays too. Although Mom, nor Dad went. I'm not implying that they were not Christian people at all; they just didn't go to church often when I was young. I was always instructed to fear and respect God. Sometimes we would go to West Baden for services, but mostly I don't think Dad liked to get dressed up. I only remember one time that he wore a tie in my life. It was on my sister's wedding day. He looked really good and so did Mom. I can still recall him saying, "I don't like 'sheep's tails.'" This was what he called dress ties. He was more comfortable in his work clothes seven days a week. Even in 1985, when we were preparing him for his funeral visitation, I recall telling the director to put the gray suit on him, but without a tie.

Every Saturday, when the weather was warm, I recall Dad on the back porch with his old, tarnished, silver, wash pan of soapy water, and shaving soap on his face, shaving his whiskers.

I don't even know if he shaved during the week, he was often up and gone or ready to go by the time I woke up. But Saturday was the big day. He smelled of Aqua Velva aftershave lotion all day. And it smelled great on him.

Later on that day we'd sit down to watch "Kentucky Afield" and then the Game of the Week that followed. I really enjoyed that.

We'd talk about the fishing show some, but it was really on to let the television warm up enough in order for us to watch the game. We really didn't care who was playing; there was always something neat about the game. I'd get so excited that I had to go back in my room and put on one of my second-hand baseball uniforms that my folks had allowed me to get at "Hilltop." "Hilltop" was like today's flea markets; it had clothes and all sorts of stuff for sale really cheap. I used to like to go there and look for baseball uniforms, spikes, stirrups, and the like. The lady that ran the place always gave me a good deal. Dad said that they got the stuff from rummage sales in Louisville and brought the stuff back to their store for poor people like us to buy. Since, it came from Louisville, I thought that the stuff really was neat. Louisville was the largest city near us and I knew that in that large of a city, there had to be some really rich people that practically wanted to get rid of their clothing. And much of the stuff looked brand new. Anyway, I enjoyed going there and finding treasures.

On the Wednesday that Joey and Mary had invited me to church, I recall being excited to be there even though I didn't know many people. It was kind of weird though because everybody seemed to know me as being Flora's little brother or Hollie and Rosie's youngest. Mom and Dad had lived in Abydell for many years and everybody seemed to know and like them. Everybody was friendly. Well, everybody except Joey. Apparently he had invited some other kids too and I hadn't thought that he would be busy with them. I was kind of alone and left to myself. I wasn't unhappy, just felt out-of-place and alone. I was considering walking home alone, but I knew that I would have had to walk home from the church and cross Highway 56. I'd have to pass Old Mrs. Elliott's house (she was a friend of my folks, although not related to us), past the Briner's house, then on along the road in front of the Maul's, the Combs', and Mr. Briner's brother's house. But I'd have to walk on around the long way to get home because I wasn't going through that tunnel in the dark! So I stayed there until youth night was over and Joey even finally had some time to talk to me. I felt okay with it all after that.

Later on, after we got a little older, I discovered that Joey also had a big brother and I liked him a lot. His name was Barry. He was really skinny, had blackish-brown hair, big white front teeth (I liked the way they looked and wished I had two front teeth just like his) and most of the time he listened when I talked to him. I also got to like Joey a lot too. We actually got to become pretty competitive in a positive way. Although soon we were all pretty close, it was Barry who was friendliest. He seemed to like to talk to Dad and that's how he got to be closer to me too. He'd ride his too-small-for-him, hand-painted, yellow bicycle down the road past our house it seemed like about twice a day, since on the way back he could fly down the hill while continuing to coast almost all the way back to the sub-station near his house. But as years went by, he'd often drive up our drive and come in and talk to Dad. To this day I cannot ever recall him ever being in my house though. Possibly, his mother told him to stay away from our house like Dad had told me to stay clear of their house. He'd sit and talk baseball with Dad and I'd listen. But whenever his mother would call out "Bar-ry" in her very distinctive cry, he'd light out on that undersized, yellow bike and down the drive way, standing up while pumping each pedal in succession to increase his speed, and down the hill he'd go. After a couple of weeks Joey also started coming over too; I was still not yet permitted to go to their house to play. But after several weeks of their visiting us, I sold Dad on the idea of my going over to their house. While there, I met the boys' dad and he was very nice, although quiet. Their mom was nice to me too. It seemed that she was especially nice to me. So after a short time, I was able to visit their house more often, providing that I had asked politely for permission. He'd say, "You can go for a little while, but you better watch out!" I never really understood where he was coming from when he said "watch out," but I guess he was just using psychology on me so that I would fear other parents and not get into any kind of trouble. He was like that, he had a sixth grade education, but must have had a PHD in psychology.

Even years after my days in Abydell, I would get the old psychology treatment when he wanted to prove a point. In fact, a state trooper friend, at Dad's funeral in 1985, told me that he had always enjoyed talking to Dad and that he had never met a more sensible man to talk with. Dad was like that, he could carry on a sensible conversation with anybody--if he wanted to.

Although I recall many times Mary would get angry at her boys for something when I was over there, she never even glanced my way. I don't know why but she never seemed to consider me as being part of the problem. So, I just stayed out of their way and hers, especially, until the smoke had passed. I always liked her, but I'm glad Dad used this psychology on me. If not, I might have gotten into trouble with her too. His was apparently a lesson on how to respect elders when visiting their homes. It must have been good advice since I never heard a negative word directed towards me from Mary or Chuck.

As for Chuck, I sometimes would go to him when Dad wasn't home because he had a bicycle tire pump and he would air up my leaky tube. It seemed that I could always find him near the road in his shed, which was attached to their garage, building something out of wood. He was a fine craftsman. He worked in a factory in Paoli. He was a taciturn man with many smiles and "yesses," but always polite and caring. I especially liked his unique appearance when he smiled. He'd widen his mouth and raise both eyebrows intuitively as he created that smile that also generated a look of surprise. He was great.

4

Harold Taught Me This

Just south of the Monon Railroad Tracks, was the oldest house in Abydell. It was the house where I lived until I was almost ten. It wasn't much to look at for most people I'd expect, but to this day I remember it as something special. I still miss the house and the small village and often find myself, especially on Christmas Eve, taking some personal time, time to ponder on how it once was. I even made a replica of the house during the fall in 2000 since the old house isn't standing anymore; I made it out of junk wood and Popsicle sticks. My parents had moved there in about 1951 and the old house was the home for my brother, Harvey, and my sister Flora Mae (she still prefers to be called "Flora"), and of course my parents Rosie and Hollie. Mom and Dad moved from Kentucky in hopes to escape hard times, but it's really hard to run from such an obscure thing as the times. However, they followed my grandparents on their move to the west--or should I say Midwest. Times must have been pretty harsh in Kentucky, since Mom and Dad just dropped everything and took off.

They lived and paid rent on that old house in Abydell for twenty-five years before we finally bought a house in Orleans, Indiana, in 1969.

This old Abydell house was constructed sometime in the 1800s and stood until 1989, when it was demolished to make room for a newer home for a new family. I recall it being hot in the summers and cold in the winters. It was constructed of poplar wood siding and tongue-in-groove walls and ceilings on the inside. Dad said that it had once been the area Post Office and trains would drop off mail there in Abydell. I don't really know how he knew this, but I recall this story. Although it was village of approximately 35 people when I live there, the town may have been a little larger. I know it once did have a country store located just north and over the tracks. All that was left of the store as far as I can remember was four broken-down sandstone walls and a few broken and splintered timbers that were once beams. Apparently there was also a country school nearby too, although there wasn't anything left of it that I recall. Our house had outlived the store mainly because of the care and sweat that my parents gave it for the quarter century. The house actually had five rooms, but we only used four of them. The fifth room, located on the southeast side contained odds and ends from the old lady that we rented from. Although we rented it from her, she had apparently been institutionalized--so we always paid an old man named Clayte Love.

Clayte was a relative of the old lady and was in charge of the house. Clayte was always a cheerful old fellow, chewing his leaf tobacco or smoking his pipe, every time I ever saw him. He would often say the same thing to me every time he saw me. As he'd look at me and think that I was really growing fast, he'd say

"'That boy will make a man before his mother will.'" He'd say this and laugh. I knew he really liked me. He was a good friend to my family for many years and he knew that the old house wasn't really much to call a home--we had an outside toilet, no running water indoors, but the best tasting water from a pump that anyone ever tasted.

I never really knew that we were poor, even when I had to take a lantern or flashlight to the outhouse in the middle of the night. It wasn't that bad because Dad had tacked up baseball cards on the spiderweb-infested walls. The cards of Clemente, Aaron, Mays, Frank Robinson, Mantle and many others were there for our reading and dreaming enjoyment. Dad was the biggest baseball fanatic anyone could ever meet. His just saying the word "BASE-Ball" was enough to make anyone know that of him. To him, baseball wasn't just the American pastime, it was what made his life useful. He was an authority on it--all aspects. He ate it, drank from it, and above all, talked it.

But I'll have to say, he never took more from it than he gave back threefold since he never talked bad about the sport, although he didn't always appreciate how some major leaguers played it. And as far as his giving back to it, he always had the time to teach any youngster anything the kid wanted to know about his game.

The first time I even considered that we were poor and some parents did not really want their kids associating with me because of it, was when I tried several times to visit another couple of neighbor kids, Ricky and Billy Combs. The boys were always friendly and we had a good time playing together--at least until their dad came home from work. In fact, I was allowed to go to their house after school let out and we would be having a great time when all of the sudden, Harold Combs came home and immediately told his boys that they had work to do and implied that I should go on home. I never really understood why he acted this way. After all, he didn't even know me. My sister used to tell me stories about all the good times she had with Sharron Combs, the boys' older sister, and Mae, their mom, when she was younger. Apparently she always felt welcome there. But for some reason I always had to go home so the boys could do their work. I really don't think they had work to do; they didn't live on a farm. They lived in the nicest house in Abydell. So at that time I wondered if there must be a connection between the fact that Harold's family had the best home and we most likely rented the least presentable house in the village. I never acted up while at the Combs'. As a matter of fact, I was really good while there. No catastrophes, no fights between the boys and me, nor among themselves--I just had to go home when Harold got home. It really hurt me. It had to be my family's lack of money, I thought. It wasn't fair that just because I was poor, I had to be set aside from friends I really liked. But, later on I also noticed that the boys really didn't get a chance to play with Barry or Joey either, and they lived directly across the road from Ricky and Billy. However, they did talk over the fence quite a bit and sometimes I saw they played a mock game of volleyball while Barry and Joey were out in the road and the Combs boys were in their own yards. But Barry and Joey didn't have a top-notch house either. It's really weird that young kids start thinking about this kind of stuff so early in life, but I remember thinking about it.

It wasn't until I became a father myself that I

began to understand possibly what Harold was all about. Now, I realize that he had been away from his kids all day at work and he probably felt that when he got home, he simply didn't want to share them with any other kids. As I got older and had kids of my own, there were times when I'd feel similarly. At times I'd think about this when my present neighbor's kids wanted to come over and play with my two little ones. I'd worry that I might be giving the wrong impression too, but there were some times when I simply didn't want to share my kids with others. Sometimes I too, made excuses to get them all to myself. However, I do allow them to play with their neighbors—but, of course they have a really nice house! Naturally, it was all in my mind that he didn't want me around. Harold and Mae have remained special friends throughout the years, and I in no way wish to imply anything negative. He simply taught me a couple of valuable lessons: The first lesson is that I need to be conscious of how my actions can be interpreted by young people. The second lesson is that I may never know who my real friends actually are until years later. After all, old friendships last the test of time.

5

The Reason I Don't Like Snakes

There were times in Abydell when I would sometimes get home from school before my parents did. I remember feeling frightened, ashamed for being frightened, and worrisome about whether Mom and Dad will get home or not. On one occasion I recall sitting on the front porch waiting for them to arrive. As I sat there near the steps, I glanced over to the pear tree. Being a little squeemish anyway since I was alone, I found myself gazing at the largest lizard I had ever seen in my life! Needless to say I scampered down the front steps, ran downhill and passed through the tunnel. I got through there so fast that I didn't even look for George and Myrtle, who supposedly lived down in the tunnel under the big boulder on the left and would get me if I played around down there, and immediately took off up the road for Barry and Joey's house. The thing was so big I recall feeling rather embarrassed as I told the Mauls about it. To this day I recall it being as big as a baby alligator. I know that this wasn't likely, but that's how I remember it.

Then on another occasion while I was once again home alone awaiting Mom and Dad's return from work, I this time suddenly got frightened about being alone. It was weird, I had been alone before, but this time I started thinking too much and decided I needed some company. During my worried state, this time I for some reason decided to go to the neighbor's back over the hill. Now this was not a good idea. But, I knew from talking to Joey that he and the rest of his family had to go to town directly after school. I didn't want to go to the Combs' house for obvious reasons, so somehow I decided to walk up the railroad tracks and then on over the hill by way of the county road. I was going to the Leathy's house. I don't know why I decided on them. But I was going. I was sad and afraid of being alone. There was no reason to be afraid, Abydell was probably the safest place on Earth. Nevertheless, I was off.

The railroad walk was a pretty quick one. The worst part of this journey was the climb up the rocky cliff just to the side of the old bridge. It was the quickest way to the road. If I didn't take this way I would need to walk nearly a half mile around the road and I wasn't going to do that. I wasn't afraid of the climb. I had done it many times before. The only problem this time was that as I was climbing up the side of the hill, I looked over under the large boulders that projected outward toward the tracks. Under a large rock there was an area that was dark, the rock underneath had been cleared out as if an animal had harbored there. But what I saw was not an opossum, not a rabbit, not a ground hog. Whatever it was, it had a large tail that flipped out and around my way as the head turned to go back into its shelter. It looked a lot like that same huge, ugly, lizard that was the size of a baby alligator! The thing's tail was huge, at least I remember it as being huge. I tried to make myself stop looking so I could climb up the bank to get to the roadway where I felt I would be safe. All the time while I was climbing and refusing to look in the thing's direction, I couldn't help but to watch it out of the corner of my eye. Fortunately, I finally made it to the road and eventually I was walking up the chip and seal road that would eventually lead down and around the corner and up again towards the neighbors. But, about half way there, I realized that I hadn't even considered whether the Leathys were even home. I started worrying then that that might be the case. I thought, "What if I walk all this way and find nobody home? . . . Their dogs are loose in the yard and they may eat me for supper." I decided to go on anyway. I walked down the winding road's hill and came upon the house. Once I got in the yard, dogs started barking and I started yelling so someone would come outside. It was a really stupid thing to do. I didn't feel comfortable there. I didn't know how they would feel about me walking all the way to their house. Luckily though, they were outside and noticed me. I was a first grader nearly in tears.

"I walked over here because Mom and Dad

were not home," I said.

"Why did you walk all this way? You shoulda called and I'd come," the mother responded.

Her remark made me feel better. And immediately I asked to use the phone to call home to see if my folks had gotten home yet. The phone rang a couple of times and Mom answered. It wasn't but a few minutes until Dad and Mom came to pick me up. Needless to say, I got a scolding. But I didn't get a whipping because I reminded Dad about the day he cracked the copperhead like a whip. I told him that I, like he did back then, knew I shouldn't have done what I had done and basically pleaded stupidity--which got me off the hook.

On another occurrence, this time while Mom was home, I was looking for a ball under Mom and Dad's bed. Mom was outside in the garden picking green beans. This was her livelihood. She loved to pick green beans, sit on the front porch swing and break them, and then cook them with a big hunk of fat-back. As I looked under the corner of the bed, I saw something wiggle and move quickly away from me. Now I had seen mice before and they did scare me a little, but this wasn't a mouse. I yelled and ran out to tell Mom. Now she had always lived out in the country and she could handle experiences like this pretty well, but I knew she wouldn't like to hear what I had to say about what I saw. Although she would kill a critter if she needed to, she would let Dad take care of the pest control if at all possible. After explaining to her what I saw, she stood right up with a mess of green beans in her apron. Her apron was where she carried the beans until she got to a bucket to use to break them. We walked on in the house and I'll have to admit, I wouldn't go back into her bedroom because I could just see that thing slithering over and crawling up my leg. Then, I heard the best news I had heard all day.

"Now you stay out here and I'll see what it is."

"Okay," I said and waited on the front porch. A few minutes later, I heard her squeal and start moving around rather fast. She opened the door of her bedroom that led to the front porch. Like many of the old houses of its time, the dwelling had two front doors. She had a broom in her hand and she was sweeping something out towards me on the porch. I heard her say, "It's a snake," as she bent forward so her feet and legs were as far away from the broom, which was wisping the critter, as possible. She looked like a hockey player moving the puck around the ice. See, to Mom, every snake was poisonous. She hated them all. I could tell that all those stories that Dad told us about Granddad were haunting her now. I too had been thinking about the story Dad had told me about when he was five. Apparently my Granddad didn't like snakes either, but the difference between him and me was that he wasn't afraid of them. As a matter of fact, I had heard stories about his catching a copperhead by the tail and cracking it like a whip. Dad said, "The head would break right off." So when Dad was five, as I had hinted earlier when I left home to find refuge at the Leathy's house, he too did a crazy thing--much worse than my leaving and walking back over the hill when I was left alone. He caught a copperhead too. He was just a small boy. He knew how to crack a whip well and he had seen his dad kill snakes this way, so he caught a snake and "cracked" the snake, killing it. But, when he proudly showed Granddad the headless snake, he said, "I got a 'whippin' that I never forgot." Well, I wasn't going to try "cracking" this snake, but my reasoning had nothing to do with getting a whipping. The next thing I knew was that she had it out on the porch, the crazy thing was wiggling, scared, and fighting back as much as it could. She swept a couple of times and down it fell off the porch and onto the ground where it wiggled some more and tried to get away. She then scurried down the steps on the other end and pulled out a hoe from underneath the house. The snake was killed right there and left laying for Dad to examine when he got home. We later found, after Dad got home, that it wasn't a poisonous snake, but he smashed its head a few more times with the hoe making sure it was forever dead.

To this day I remember the huge lizards and the snake at Abydell and I still don't like them. It has always been in my mind that if I see a snake and don't kill it, I just might find it under the bed sometime. Most people have never had this feeling, but they would have had it if they grew up in the old Abydell house.

6

Silhouettes At Night

Late at night, while I was still awake, I would
hear the train whistles blaring down on our
small community. They sounded as if they
were running a hundred miles per hour. After
the engine had made its way past our front
yard, I always would watch from my bed the
front room end table lamp as it seemed to
have something mysterious and eerie happen.
Sometimes I would watch for a few seconds
and then cover my head in fright. I liked it,
I didn't feel that the occurrence was anything
that would endanger me, but still it was strange.
I saw the silhouettes of small beings entering

our house. I made believe so well that somehow this gave me goose bumps similar to my visitation to the tunnel. I made these shapes real; they were mine and until now I never told anyone about them. As I look back, it was really fun to make-believe in this manner. I suppose all young kids enjoyed being afraid sometimes. This was my way at night. I had toys to play with when I was awake, but when I was in bed, this was a sort of eerie game I played on myself. In actuality it was the movement of leaves being swished back and forth from the wind of the passing train cars. Somehow this action projected a flashing light through the windows that looked just like small shapes running to our front room's end table lamp. I knew what it actually was, but I somehow enjoyed thinking that they were train beings stopping in to check things out each night. I never spent much time wondering why these shadows always wandered over to the lamp. In my imagination these were silhouettes that left the train near the engines and ran quickly into the house and left just in time to catch the caboose. On the other hand, I was so used to hearing the train that when I had fallen asleep, I cannot ever remember it waking me from my sleep. Even when we moved to Orleans near the summer of 1969, I cannot recall waking up when the train passed by our house and we lived close to the tracks there too. However, I cannot ever recall making believe that the silhouettes ever visited the Orleans house. It was home to me for about nine years until I moved off to attend college. I suppose that my imagination was at its best when I lived in Abydell. I suppose it had to be because I had to create ways to have fun.

7

Down by the Branch

Growing up in Abydell was simple; the times
we had were special, especially on the weekends when my sister, Flora and her husband,
John came to visit. John was always my best
friend while growing up. He always had time
to talk with me and was always willing to in-
clude me in anything he was doing. In fact, the
day they were married he even was willing to
take me along on their honeymoon I heard later on from my sister. I don't know if this was
really true, but this is what Flora told me later
on. She said that as I cried when they made
their way out of the church, he looked over at

her and commented, "'Well let him in; he can go.'" He was sort of a teacher too. It seemed no matter what the two of us were doing, he was patient and explained the goings-on to me. Plus, I can't ever remember one time growing up when he pressured me to believe anything. Instead, he would explain the situation and let me come to my own conclusions. This is why I think of him as being my first real teacher. My being a teacher had a great deal to do with his tutoring me. His patience and caring and enthusiasm were inspirational in my younger years.

My first recollection of John visiting our house to court my sister is when he would ride his Harley Davidson over wearing his black leather jacket that had dice chains and zipper pulls on it. He would always have caramel candy squares that he would share with me. I recall mentioning this to him this past year and he insists that I had to be remembering someone else that visited my sister. He doesn't remember the candy at all. I know it was him and I thought that was great. It was also great to get to take a ride with him on his Harley--often there were three of us on the bike at one time! Throughout the years he was always there for me and is still a good person--Flora made a good choice.

Some of the best times I recall is when our family had wiener and marshmallow roasts down in the branch at our house. In the front yard of our property we had a branch where after it would rain, the water would wind and rush down through the tunnel under the railroad tracks. Dad and I seemed to have the most fun playing in the water after a hard summer rain, but when the branch was dry, the sandstone pebbles made a great place to build a fire for a cookout. We didn't have a fancy grill in those days, and I can't remember ever cooking anything like hamburgers outdoors at our house--hamburgers wouldn't stay on a stick like hot dogs or marshmallows. Dad or John would show me how to get the fire going and then help me cut and gather green limbs from nearby trees to use as sticks for the hot dogs. I liked my dogs burnt and so did my sister. Everyone else was a little more careful to get the dogs "medium done," gourmet style. Then, we would slap them on a bun and some would pour on ketchup, but I used mustard on mine and I still can't take mine any other way. Ketchup was for hamburgers and mustard was for hot dogs or sometimes a ham sandwich. It was a great time that usually ended with a game of basketball down in the bottom on an old goal that had a round pumpkin-shaped bank board. It really was pumpkin-shaped. And orange too. As a matter of fact, I remember helping John and Dad put it up and insisting that the writing show on the outside rather than on the back. Dad had somehow gotten it while working on the highway. He was a highway department worker. The sign itself had been a sign that advertised the Pumpkin Festival in French Lick-West Baden. It was perfect I thought for putting up a basketball goal. It read something like: "Pumpkin Festival October 24-29, French Lick, Indiana." Today, as I look back, I should have turned the writing to the back. Most of the time it was John and I playing basketball on the old goal, but sometimes Dad would join us and shoot his "granny-grunt" shots--he never moved around much on offense, and never played any defense. But if you'd let him set up somewhere out at the top of the key area and wait until he was passed the ball, he'd "can it" more times than not. John, on the other hand, really tried to make me a good player by instructing me on shooting techniques and playing defense and offense. When I played one-on-one with John, I can remember not being able to stop laughing when he guarded me. I don't know why, but any time he would get close to me when I had the ball I'd just crack up giggling. He would try to keep a straight face too and ask me "What are you gonna do when someone guards you in a real game? You gotta stop laughing to score." Later on, I found that I only laughed when John guarded me.

Other times I'd bug Dad or John to play baseball, which was my real love, so much that they'd finally give in and play "pitch and catch." Now it was Dad this time that would do the instructing. He'd fungo me fly balls and tell me to do things like "get your feet lined up right to make the catch and throw the ball back to me on one hop." He never liked to have to chase the ball--I was instructed early to make good throws by the man I still call the master. I still bet this old man could still handle the bat up until the day he died. We'd play pepper and he could hit the ball if he could reach it just about anywhere he wanted to every time. As a matter of fact, many years later in Orleans, I was playing Babe Ruth League Baseball for a coach named Danny Clark, who was my very first good, but tough, higher level coach. That day Danny brought out a pitching machine for us to learn how to hit the curve ball. We never had an opportunity to use a "Jugs" brand pitching machine in practice and in fact, the only other pitching machine I had ever seen was early in the 70s. It was located in Orleans on Main Street right across from my friend, Jay Strauss's house. I think it was owned and operated by Bud Barley, a nice man who coached a little league team I played against there. Anyway, Danny got in there after none of my teammates could hit the ball with any authority or consistency. He swung at several pitches and didn't make contact with the ball--he didn't look much better than the rest of us. Dad stood back behind the backstop and sort of laughed at Coach--they were friends and Coach Danny wasn't seriously offended by my old man's chuckles. Possibly, because Danny knew (in his mind) that if he couldn't hit it, the old man (Dad) couldn't either. After a few minutes of Dad's jeering and of course, instructional advice on how Danny should hit the breaking pitch, he held the bat out towards Dad and calmly said, "Okay, old man come in here and show me what you can do!" Boy I was really embarrassed, Dad was about 62 at the time; I wasn't sure I wanted to be seen with him coming onto the field and making himself look stupid by not hitting a single pitch. In my mind I could just hear the kids laughing at him and teasing me after all of his jeering at Danny, when he looked silly. But at the same time, I was frustrated with not hitting the curve ball too. Dad kept telling me too that I had to "stay in there and hit the ball where it's pitched and let the ball get to you and hit it the other way." He said this over and over and seemed a little frustrated that I didn't handle the machine, so I was pretty near the point of saying, "Why don't you try it if you think it's so easy?" Well Dad took on Coach's challenge. He walked in, picked up the first bat that was close to him, spit some tobacco juice on his hands, and said "Shoot me one so I can see it once." He hit one line drive to right! One line drive to left field. And then proceeded to hit a shot right back at Danny, whose eyes enlarged as big as Kennedy half-dollars as he dove out from behind the machine he was feeding! Then, Dad laid the bat down and quietly walked off. Never did he say another word. And neither did Danny have anything to say either. My teammates smiled at him with the utmost respect. This was the only time I ever saw my dad as a hero. Dad had always seemed old to me. In fact, he was fifty years old when I was born. Needless to say, he was way past his prime. By no means could he do everything he used to be able to do as a player, but that day I could tell that he once was a better-than-average ball player. That was a special day for him too. It was the day he showed his son that he had more than just a fundamental knowledge of the game.

In Abydell when we played games in the yard, it was usually with a plastic whiffle ball. I remember not wanting to be paired up with Dad as a teammate. I loved him and respected him tremendously, but he was just too old to bend down and pick up a ground ball and he couldn't catch that silly whiffle ball like he could a baseball. But down across the branch where we'd have our hot dog roasts, we'd get a game going. I took it seriously. I wanted to play like a pro. We'd usually have one on a team, and Dad would be "all time pitcher"--this means that he'd pitch to both, or all three teams. He could do that very well, as far as throwing strikes. But he couldn't cover his position very well. See most of the time, the pitcher would have to pitch and after the ball is hit, he'd have to cover first base too. The field was laid out so that the pitcher's mound was not far from first base, since it was a narrow field that got wider past first and third. I got so aggravated when I'd pick up the ball and make what I thought was a spectacular throw to Dad covering first and he just couldn't come up with it. Usually it was the family playing the game, but often Barry and Joey would arrive and want to get in too. Then we'd play two-on-two with Barry and Dad playing against Joey and me. Later on was when we came up with the idea to play three separate teams. We had to use "ghost runners" on bases after a runner was safe. Then the same person went back to bat again until three outs were made. Barry was more patient with Dad than I was--he played simply for amusement. Joey and I were out for blood! We'd always make believe that we were actually major leaguers. I'd bat through the Mets line up. I'd first imagine I was Tommie Agee, then Wayne Garrett, then Cleon Jones and so on until I went all the way through the whole line up. Joey would always be the Big Red Machine as he'd imagine he was Rose, Morgan, Bench, Perez and so on. Barry then got involved in this and he was always the St. Louis Cardinals. He loved the Cardinals. In fact, he started listening to them on the radio as he put his baseball cards in a batting order while listening. Later on, he created games and rolled dice. He may have been the original creator of baseball board games. Not only did he use his baseball cards for his board game; he even made up a neighborhood dog baseball team! I noticed though that he always cheated with the stats because his dog (Lobo) was always the star. My dog (Cocoa) played second base and was more of a slash and dash hitter, according to Barry.

As I look back I know that Dad did the best he could and I loved having him play with us down in the bottom. I only wish I had had more patience with his play. After all, he was the most patient man with me when it came to baseball that I had ever seen. It wasn't until later in Orleans when Danny Clark's Babe Ruth All Star team was trying to hit that "Jugs" machine that I truly recognized that he was once a great player. But all the time playing in Abydell, in the back yard, up until I was about ten and later on in high school and college, he remained patient with his teaching of the game of baseball, even though he couldn't catch that crazy whiffle ball in Abydell! Dad was my baseball mentor and John was my teacher for basketball. Those days in Abydell and later on in Orleans, were days I'll never forget. No matter whether I was gathering sticks for a family hot dog roast with Dad or John near the branch on the outskirts of my "Whiffle Ball Stadium," or whether I was gathering knowledge from the two most important male teachers in my early life, I enjoyed those times.

8

Winter Time Was Basketball Time in Indiana

Everybody in the Midwest knows that basketball season never ends. But for Dad it was when the World Series is over. Then and only then was it basketball time. See, for Dad, it was basketball time only because there was no baseball to watch. So without baseball, he had to settle for watching WTTV Channel 4 out of Indianapolis. This channel showed Indiana University Basketball and Purdue University Basketball, but I suppose in actuality he was a University of Kentucky follower first. He had to watch Channel 3 or Channel 11 out of Louisville to get Wildcat games.

Personally, the first time I can recall getting excited about basketball was when I was in Mrs. Apple's third grade class at French Lick. Even at home after watching basketball on television for a short time, I'd eventually have to run off to the back room to shoot a few shots at a bottomless cardboard box that I had stuck up over the door. I somehow made it stay up there without putting any nails in the wall by leaving a lip on the back of the box and jamming it in behind the trim over the door. I think that is the only way I could play at home during the winter months. But during the day at school, Mrs. Apple, would take us down to the gymnasium at the elementary school for recess. I can recall being particulary good at long shots and hitting "swooping," fast-break lay ups. I wonder what happened to me when I was in high school because I recall missing a few wide open lay ups in varsity games! My loving to play inspired several of my third grade classmates to play too. At the time they were not as accomplished as I was, but by the time I played against them in high school, when I moved to Orleans, they surely had caught up with me. During recess, I was so inspired that I started dressing in the locker room and practiced running out onto the court. I had asked some of the other guys to dress out soon thereafter, but they commented that they didn't have gym shorts. So, I figured one weekend that at Hill Top I would look for them some practice gear too. I did and brought these hand-me-down shorts and shirts to school. All the boys wore the attire and our running out on the court soon inspired the girls to begin cheerleading when we entered to court. It wasn't long before the girls were making Pom Poms and working on cheers as we played. Never did we ever need a referee, nor did we ever get into an argument or fight. It was so awesome for us to get along so well. We had a blast and Mrs. Apple soon got into the games too and I noticed that she'd even clap when we made baskets. I watched her watch us and as a teacher; she was there to supervise the whole class, but I know she watched the game more than she watched the other kids playing tag or whatever. She even took us down to the gym a few times when we were the only class there. She knew that she was doing us just as much good in this activity as she was teaching math and English!

A Revelation: Winter was Coming to an End

However, one day in Abydell, I believe it was the middle of March, as my family returned home from shopping in Bedford, I noticed for the first time in my life that winter was over. Never before had I ever remembered even thinking about the seasons changing. I suppose I was growing up; I had realized that spring was coming. I guess it had always just happened. I don't remember. But,this day the weather was noticeably warmer than it had been. The water was not frozen in the branch nor inside the house. See, sometimes in the old house on very cold nights, the water bucket we drank from in the kitchen had a thick frozen layer of ice. But on this day, as I got out of my sister's yellow 1967 Impala, I could see that the snow was nearly melted on the yard. The thawing of the snow on the roof had caused a constant dripping action that I had never noticed before. It was a whole new world for me to see. As I walked towards the front porch I now heard the melted snow water as it ran through the branch before spilling over the large rock into the tunnel. It was a great sound! There was no way I was going inside. I had to stay out and look around for more signs of spring. Then I noticed a few green sprouts of grass here and there and some brightly colored new buds on the trees beginning to show. And there were birds singing like I'd never heard before. They seemed to be having a family reunion as each one made its own special sound. And like most friendly reunions, every "old bird" was chattering at the same time. With all of this happening unexpectedly, I soon had my basketball in my hands (it had laid out under the goal since November). While listening to all the new sounds, I began shooting at the old pumpkin backboard. I still couldn't dribble the ball (even it had air in it) because the ground was so soft, but I could shoot the old, muddy ball. After a few shots though, I found that I had to quickly rebound the ball off the rim before it "splatted" on the muddy ground. This was just enough to me get ready for the next day's games at recess.

9

A Painful Dream, but I didn't Care

Many years had passed since I played down in the bottom, whether it was whiffle ball in the summer or basketball in the winter or spring. Eight years to be exact since the last time I played there. I was revisiting the old homestead, although the house was nearly falling down and raccoons and squirrels most likely had taken over the premises within the walls. I pulled into the driveway slowly, looked down the lane to the old house and reminisced about how it used to be and wondered whether it was normal for a young person my age to yearn for what used to be. I had often wondered this.

In fact, I recall not wanting to move away. But of course back then I was curious about what was ahead of me and this question allowed me to help pack up my belongings and head for Orleans where I would finish out my elementary, junior high and high school years. As I stepped out of my parent's 1969 Buick Skylark into what was once the front yard and walked up to the front steps, the memories started rekindling again. The longed for feelings I had once felt in the spring when I could hear the branch running. I missed the cold snap of winter. I listened for any signs of these as I took each step toward the front of the porch. I was consumed by the summer's heat and the vast aroma of the weeds and the sound of bees buzzing in the pear tree just in front of the porch. Then all of the sudden all of these came back to me in a whirlwind of odors and sounds. From the air I especially tasted the rot of old wet and dried mud that laid underneath the porch. My family and I had certainly contributed to all of those smells that were apparent. Many a warm summer evening had I walked out on the front porch and relieved myself over the rail since we had no indoor facilities. There was no urine smell now nor then, but I'm sure I had contributed to the sweet odor. As I turned around the front door looked quiet and sad as it hung latched. The screen door was completely gone. Although shadowed and faded, I noted the circular Mets insignia that Dad had so candidly placed on the door's glass so many years ago. I wondered why anyone would ever put a baseball insignia on the front door, but Dad often put things in most peculiar places. A kind of knack he had, I guess. It was a pathetically humorous way to put his mark on his world. I then turned the knob slowly and actually had to lift up on the knob with both hands to separate the door from the years of being shut. It finally opened freely and simply to a dark living room. To the left, the floor sloped a little downward to where the chimney still stood. It always did, I recalled. The opening to where the stovepipe once attached so perfectly to the painted brick was drooling mildewed soot. It appeared to be begging for someone to clean it out one last time or at least patch it over. The bricks were hanging as if they were merely there because the paint and soot somehow held them together. Looking towards the back wall of the front room and to the left of the doorway to the kitchen was the broken remains of what was once the doorway to my parents' bedroom. This is where I would envision those silhouettes of the friendly people visiting our house at night when the train passed. The doorway was impassible now, but as I pulled aside a board to make my way through, I heard a tremendous screech of settling in the whole middle portion of the building. It scared me a bit, but I had heard settling before and continued to make my way through. Then came a "Screech, SCR-eee-ch" and "snap!" But the snap was not only a sound; it was a feeling too because something hit me sharply on the back of the neck. From this I recall I was somewhat dazed and puzzled. Apparently something happened to me that had never happened before. I, for some unknown reason, felt a strangeness that I had been here before. Not here in the house I had grown up in, but a house that I had known before I knew my parents. It seemed that I now recalled growing up here in this house but I also had another recollection of another time. It was the feeling that I had been there before the time I had actually lived there!

A time that did not make any sense to me. A time when the house itself looked newer than the time when my family had been in habitation. In fact, a different type of building did I recall--A time when the place had been established as a business for taking and passing on mail. Then for some reason I experienced an urge to chase down a white horse in the side yard. I heard one of the workmen on the soon-to-become railroad yell, "'Hey the white horse has broken loose and it's making its way towards the store.'" I heard at least one additional voice as another worker called for water. I heard this over and over until finally, I realized that I had been knocked unconscious and all of this was a dream that I had been experiencing as I lay on the dry dusty floor.

"Roger, time to get ready for school," came from Mom's voice.

"Whew! I replied to myself as I crawled lazily out of my bed in Orleans.

10

"The Whip"

During a Christmas party my wife had cooked up with our friends in 2005, Greg Gordon and I stole away to my office to look at a new laptop computer that I had recently purchased. Well, this was the reason this time to get away. It was not long before we began talking about writing. Greg was already a published writer and I had been teaching high schoolers to write for many years. In fact, I was teaching his son, Josh, English at that time. As he sat down in the guest chair in my den, I nestled into my desk chair. He then commented how his son had enjoyed my class and that he often too longed to go back and take his high school grammar courses. Specifically he said, "'When we are young, we don't care about grammar, but now I would love to take a class again.'" I was sure that he was just being nice since he had already written two books that I knew of. I assumed that he had had at least one teacher who inspired him to write. Shoot, I really didn't know what I could teach him. So, soon we began talking about what Josh had been learning and he commented again that he needed to know more about grammar. Earlier, when we were downstairs with all of our other friends, he had commented on the amount of time it must have taken me to build the replica of the old Abydell house. He had seen it a couple of years earlier on a previous visit. I said, that it took a good while, but I enjoyed the time because it allowed me to rekindle some old memories. After a short pause, I mentioned that Josh had been studying commas and adjectives in my class most recently. Then when Greg asked me about what I had picked up along my way that would directly improve a writer. Again, I didn't feel that I could help him. Heck, I still didn't really and truly know why I was writing about my times in Abydell. However, I dug deep and commented, "Well, everyone talks about description and the use of adjectives. I have found one thing recently," I said. "I have come to find that everybody talks about the adjectives, but what really makes good description is the adverbs that are set just before the adjectives." He then asked me to offer an easy explanation.

"What, again, is it that adjectives are supposed to do?" he asked.

"I'm sure that you know that adjectives modify or help describe nouns or subjects. But I have found that these adjectives are more descriptive when they are preceded by a well chosen adverb, a word that may modify or describe the adjective. But this can be overdone too."

"Overdone?"

"Yes, to make it simple for a guy who's not been in high school English for a while, think of a subject. Then, pick a word to describe your subject (an adjective). Then, next choose a word that will describe the adjective. This adverb that describes the adjective can add a great deal to your descriptive prose. But, I've learned if this is done merely to fill space on paper, it merely becomes just that...a filler."

"Okay, I see," commented Greg.

"See, the average writer tries to re-create a vision he's writing about with mere adjectives. He can have more if, and only if, the need is warranted. Many times the adjective is suffice," I said.

"Yeh, and isn't it amazin' how just hearing an old song forces you to think?"

"Recreating with adjectives and adverbs--that's about all I know that I might offer as a consideration to writers."

"Yes, we love to recreate," joked Dr. Gordon.

"No, I meant to say re-create! I just didn't place enough emphasis on the hyphen. Sorry."

We both chuckled about my word choice because we both recognized how the word obviously was awkwardly ambiguous.

"But on a more serious note, I especially enjoy reminiscing during the holiday season; I don't always need all of the hoopla of celebration to enjoy the holidays. And as for parties, I enjoy small parties. More specifically, I would have to say that I enjoy one-on-one conversation better. But, I do love thinking back at how it use to be.

--But, maybe I'm living too much in the past," I said.

"I have a friend that is very similar. . . ," Greg told me as he was insinuating that he, himself was that friend. Since I could tell he was referring to himself and while he was explaining himself here, I jutted in, "Is your friend crazy too?"

"I hope not," he laughed.

"As I said a minute ago, have you ever noticed how just the hearing of an old song brings back memories where you can recall things that you've forgotten for years? —Memories of where you were when you heard it and who you were with?"

"Oh, I know," I said. And just as that came out of my mouth and without any song to make me reminisce, something made me look up and over to the right of where he was sitting. For some reason what he had said made me think about something that used to be up there on my shelving. It was so real that I just had to look to see if it was there. I knew it had been long removed from this spot to the living room closet. This object immediately became so intriguing that I just had to go get it and share with him what it was and what made it so special to me.

"Come on, I want to show you something that is nearly as old as I am."

We both took off to the front porch.

"Have you ever cracked a whip?"

"Yes, I have," he said without hesitation.

"Well, let me rephrase. --Has anyone ever showed you how to crack a whip properly?"

"No, but I know how to crack a whip."

"Well, my dad was very good with a whip... he was the one who told me that 'a girl cracks a whip like this.'" I then showed him how most people attempted the task. And then went on to say that Dad would not allow me to do it improperly.

"Yeah, that's the way I would have cracked it," chuckled Greg.

"Just flipping it up and then down to crack it, is not what Dad would have approved of. Instead, he said to do it like this."

Then, I showed what the old master had showed me. "Up, around, and then out front."

"CRACK!" Went the whip in the cool winter air as the sound ricocheted off the house across the way.

"Let me try. . . So its up, around, and crack." But, the crack occurred back behind him, rather than out front. He tried again and again with the same outcome.

"Think of it like snapping off a curve ball. Snap it out front!" I said, because I knew he had been a pitcher back in high school. I thought that that analogy would cause success. But, it didn't. He needed Dad to teach him. Then I proceded to tell him:

"I gotta tell you, I got this whip for a fifty cent piece when I was about six or seven years old.

"Really," he commented.

"Yes, when I was younger, on Saturday mornings I would follow along with my dad to the old West Baden Sale Barn."

I then glanced at him to see if he was interested in hearing an anecdote and it appeared that he did.

"Go ahead. Go on . . . ."

"Well sometimes on Saturdays, Dad went to watch and pick up a few bargains there and I always enjoyed going too. But one day, I got a little bored while the sale was going on and went outside the newly built barn and proceeded towards the old worn-out barn. This was still where the concession stand was located. On my way over I found the old barn still being used for live-stock. As I made my way around the cattle and goats to get to the concession stand, I smelled the hot dogs in the distance. Well, I knew I had to have one with mustard. So, I entered and immediately heard the screen door slam behind me. I can still recall that there was an old Colonial Bread sign on the door about handle high. Inside the room, there was a long "U-shaped" bar with ten or twelve stools where people sat and ate. It smelled great in there. . . couldn't even smell the animal odors once inside.

"Go on."

"This is where I got this whip."

"You got it in the concession stand?"

"No there was a boy who had this very whip and he was sporting it around like a new toy . . .like a toy that had just promoted him from a kid to an adult. And he had a following too. His buddies were with him, one on each side of him and a little guy following them, too. They walked proud. You could just tell how big and important they all felt."

"So, how did you get the whip?"

"Like I said, I had a brand new, shiny, fifty-cent piece in my pocket and after a few minutes I flashed it in the direction of the boy with the whip. He seemed to lose all respect for the whip when he saw that much money. I could tell I had a chance to get that whip. Fifty cents."

"Well, do you remember what you said to him and what he said to you?"

"Yes, it was like this: 'Hey, kid,' the boy said as he seemed to feel older than I was because he held the whip. He may have been older than me by a year or two, but the whip made him feel like a teenager ready to become a man. His buddies already felt he was a man."

"'Huh?' I answered, acting as if I had not even noticed his whip. My answer was merely a priming of the pump. My answer sounded perfect. It showed absolutely no interest in the boy or his fine whip."

"I see you have a coin there," he said.

"Oh, this? Yeah, it's a brand new fifty cent piece."

"'Let's see it,' he said as he winked at his buddies."

"'I guess,' I replied."

"Then, what came out of his mouth was absolutely amazing. It was my lucky day. I was shaking, but couldn't let on. He said, 'How about tradin'?'"

"'What do ya have?' I said as if I had no idea of what he had."

"Remember, I wanted it badly! But never let on."

"'I got this.' He said as he took the leather from his shoulder. He was wearing it like a banner draping around his neck and hanging tightly down around his cowboy belt. He had boots too. He had it all. Cowboy hat, belt, and the whip."

"Before I could think of anything clever to say, I blurted, 'Okay, it's a d-deal.' He had to hear the quiver in my voice. But, apparently, he was as proud to get my half dollar as I was to get his bull-whip! Maybe the quiver in my voice made him feel that he'd just taken advantage of me."

"We exchanged and immediately went our ways. I didn't even take time to try it out. I was getting away with the deal of the century."

"Well, good for you."

"But Greg, I want you to know that I had to

fight that kid later that day because someone told him that I had taken advantage of him."

"Oh, yeah? How did that go?"

"Well, I have the whip don't I?"

"Yea, you do."

"I have it and later on I traded it to my dad because he loved it more than I did. . . .I can't even remember what I traded him for—I think it was three dollars."

"So, that was it, then. This is the whip that you had when you lived in Abydell."

"Yep, and I recall that his grandma, who was the secretary at the sale barn wasn't very happy with his deal, but she told him that a man must stand behind his deal and that was that. I heard her say this myself as Dad talked to her about the deal and the situation that had taken place. I also remember her saying, 'Well, he'll learn.' . . .Meaning that her grandson will have to learn from this incident."

Later on, after Greg and the rest of our Christmas guests had gone home, I realized that I couldn't have written this chapter without his prompting. I found a new angle.

11

Christmas Eve

Many times had our family revisited Abydell since we moved away. We had friends there and my brother, Harvey still lived in the village with his wife. While my parents visited with my brother one Christmas Eve I stole away as I often did to walk the drive that led to the old house. Often I'd visit my friends who still resided in the community to play football because it was the outdoor sport of winter. But this time I didn't invite anyone to go along. I wanted to go home alone. It had been my plan to walk through the old tunnel once more, but instead for some reason I can't remember now,

I walked around the corner and up the road and then across the tracks to enter near the old mailbox. It was still there alone, surrounded only by tall weeds. We didn't take it when we moved—I guess because in town we didn't need such a big mailbox. After all, the mail came right to our front porch on East Jefferson Street. Another reason Dad didn't take it along was because it was a fixture. Heck, it probably was there when Mom and Dad moved there. It was just something that should stay. It was a part of the house's being. It should've stayed. I wasn't even sure it would've come down from the post after 25 years without disintegrating into mere particles of rust. And as I approached it, I wondered how many times my parents had walked out to get the mail, how many times they had stopped the car at the end of the drive in order to get the mail . . . Too many to count, for sure. The lane itself was just as it once was except for the grass being taller in the center where the tire tracks didn't wear it down. Undoubtedly, I felt that the gravel lane was going to be there, hard and ready to use for a couple hundred years, whether anyone used it or not. In fact, I recall thinking it was nearly as hard as the chip and seal county road it joined. Walking towards the old house that once was our home, I noted just behind me a strange car using the drive as a turn around. I could see the old home plainly from its headlights. The lights shone brightly on the west of the house and a gleam appeared on the front room window. Once where there was a security light on the front electric pole, there was only darkness as the car's light disappeared. Except for the light from the stars overhead, there was darkness everywhere. The house, now lonely and even more dilapidated than years past, sat quietly, sad and cold and it was painful to see what was once the center of my universe dissolved as the darkness took hold once again after the car's lights left the stage. Gone was the cheer we once shared.--Nothing was left but the ghosts of past life dwelling thereabouts. It was Christmas Eve, but I was taken in by the loneliness I felt. It was a loneliness that would never again be dissolved.

The times we had were dear and even though we were physically gone from the home, it was still precious in me. While standing upright, I rested my head straight back and somehow saw myself as a child peeking from the front window as I often did to see if someone was coming up the driveway. This was also the place I'd watched for the bus in the morning since I could see it coming towards the bus stop, as it hurried down the distant hill nearly a half mile away. Once I had seen it through the window, I had just enough time to pick up my heavy books and hand-me-down coat before running as fast as I could to get to the end of the driveway. I can recall that the bus would always arrive just before me. The driver would blow the horn and give me an agitated look if I was not ready to board when he got there. But now, there was no father out front chopping kindling; no kind mother's love coming from the light-less kitchen now as she prepared a simple, but filling meal. However, I still was able to rekindle a memory of Christmas Eve. The cold air, the falling snow, our dressing for a long walk to get a special Christmas tree which became the center of my family's experience.

12

Christmases I Miss

While living in Abydell, I don't believe I can ever recall my parents buying a tree for Christmas. But, I can easily recall walking from the warm front room just after soaking up as much heat as possible from the wood stove. I can still remember the smell of the wood burning and the heat singe it made on my clothing. This heat was so hot that my clothing became hot to the touch. Sometimes the cuffs of my coat were actually scorched. In fact I recall looking at my clothing to see if anything was on fire. And often did I have to walk straight legged because my pants were so hot that I felt I had to keep them from touching my skin. When full and after heating for a long while, the stove became red hot. That heat stayed with me almost until I got to the wood pile. Then it felt hard and stiff like clothing after starching. Afterward the warmth gave way to the cold air and as I continued to walk, my exercised, sweaty legs kept the pant legs warm until they gave way to the freeze.

Dad and I had a special place to find a tree. To get there we needed to walk down to the tunnel and up the side of the hill near the huge rock that overhung the opening of the tunnel. From there we'd take a right walking East on the railroad tracks. Of course, we could have driven around the road and pulled off and left the car just off the road, but that was wasteful and seemed lazy even if gasoline was plentiful I don't recall wasting anything in Abydell (except for the summer when I took Mom's sack of flour out to the whiffle ball field to make a batters box and foul lines). Dad walked the timbers of the tracks while he kept an eye on how long I could stay atop the rails walking with my already cold hands balancing my body like a tight roper I'd only seen on TV. Approaching the bridge where I once climbed to get to the roadway when I was scared because nobody was home with me, I gazed at the wooden beams that held up the bridge because they were there and I just couldn't keep my eyes fixed on the rails too long. Although cold and boredom had set in, I was happy to be young and carefree. It was just beyond this bridge that we would take off to the right into the woods. Not left, because that was the way to Pope's Pond, where Uncle Jack and Dad often took me fishing in the summers and always heard the Bob White calls from the distance. No, the trees were to the right. Never did we ever go to the right together in the winter except for the times we'd hunt for that special Christmas tree. However, we did hunt mushrooms there in the spring because Dad always said they grew best under pine trees. But, it was winter now and the evening before Christmas. We had a special job to do and must get it done before the family got together tonight. Mom and Dad always had their hearts set for the Pine tree, but I had seen a cedar tree at the neighbor's and I liked it fine. Flora had told me that she and Dad used to cut cedars when she was younger. In fact, it

was from the exact area. But as far as I can recall, we'd never had a cedar in our house. After
stepping off of the railroad and onto the bank
entering the wooded area, we'd entered a darker
world-- world of brown, dead weeds, annoying
cockleburs, and wild tree growth. Dad'd use his
ax to brush away the limbs before they swiped
across our faces. I usually picked up a partially
barked stick to use for my own needs. We'd
walk up the slight embankment and upward
around the hollow to enter the pine grove. Most
of the trees were cedars, so we'd have to look
some to find what we wanted. There weren't
many pines, and of the pines we'd find, most
were one-sided or much too sparse between
the branches because they were tall. Dad'd always say that that was the problem with cutting
one's own tree. "There are a lot of trees, but
not many good ones." I knew from an early age
that he'd rather get a one-sided tree that would
better fit up against the wall than to get one
that is too sparse. But, he knew Mom would
prefer a round one. Before long, he'd decide
on one and show it to me. It would be a tall
tree, but he would say, "We'll just top it." Well,
after climbing the tree and after about 25 or

30 chops, the top would lean downward and in my direction. Of course, I would be told to move out of its way. I'd skidaddle just in time to watch it fall the rest of the way down. It'd glance off of one lower limb and onto another before swishing to the dried, cold leaves on the ground. Only the trunk of what had been cut would made a "thunk" as it contacted the cold ground. I'd always think it would be a fine tree and I couldn't wait to get it home. I'd think it was getting more like Christmas since we had a tree. After Dad climbed back down, he'd throw it back over his shoulder. He knew just how to steady it with one forearm. He'd then pick up the ax he'd rested on his leg and we'd take out for home. I would never know who owned the land where we'd find the tree, but I'm sure Dad knew and I'm also sure he had permission to get a tree there. We were all friends around there.

Getting impatient about getting home I'd have started walking with one foot on and one foot off the tracks nearly all the way home. I would always remember going to get the tree, but it's funny that I can't remember anything about the way home. Nor could I ever recall being cold or bored on the way back. My mind would have been on getting back as quickly as possible.

Back home before taking the tree into the house, we'd get out the saw from under the front porch and cut the trunk straight across. I'd get to saw only after Dad got the blade started straight. Next, we'd saw off the ends of two sticks; Dad'd always have a few nicely planed sticks that he'd picked up somewhere to make the "X". The "X" was used for a base. Then, after cutting a couple of small three-inch pieces for leveling purposes-- they'd be tacked onto the stick already nailed to the trunk. Then we were careful to nail it all together. This process was used year-after-year and for the most part, it leveled it pretty well before we took it inside.

While we were gone Mom had gone back into the back room and retrieved the ornaments that were safely put away in a cardboard box. There were lights from previous years that she'd have to change bulbs from one string to another in order to get enough to light the tree. Of course she'd also have to borrow an extension cord from some place in the house because we only had two electrical plugs in the front room. After stretching out each light set to see which one had the most lights that would light, she'd start wrapping the tree, stringing it up and down for the best overall coverage. Dad would always feel that he had to go over the stringing himself because Mom wouldn't get it right. Next, we'd all add an ornament to just the right location. Then, we'd attach the rest of the trimmings. Some years we'd have icicles to throw around the tree making sure that they would droop down exactly like real ice would look. These icicles were actually made of shredded silver wrapping paper and they were nearly impossible to make look bad. Also popular was the snow that we would purchase from Wilson Roberts at his store in Paoli. The store was called the Variety Store and it was great. It was located on the North side of the square right across from the courthouse and next to Norman's Clothing Store. The Variety Store was the ultimate store for toys. It had everything I wanted and Mom wouldn't have to shop anywhere else to purchase everything. Often, I recall going in with her and I'd be so consumed by looking at the toy tractors and

122 trucks and basketballs and baseball gloves that she could pick out all of my presents in less than one hour and I never even saw her pick one up. I never even saw her check out! All I knew was that she'd carry a bag out of the store and I didn't ever care about looking in the bag. When I was young, I was always told not to look under Mom's bed. Shoot, after I found that snake the previous summer under there, I didn't have any desire to peek under the bed for any reason. So, for the most part I didn't look for the presents. Besides, I really didn't want to know what I was getting or I'd spoil my surprise. But, I do recall one occasion while playing in the floor in Mom's bedroom I could see some wrapped gifts under the bed. Well, I felt ashamed and stopped looking. On another occasion I found one Christmas present in this location and it was nearly Spring time. Mom'd forget to give me one sometimes and it would lay under that bed until it was found. We'd all have a good laugh and afterwards she'd allow me to open it. One year though, when I was a little older, I guess she thought I was too old and she needed to find a better hiding place. Then a present was found in the

back of Dad's old Studebaker truck. Actually it was my little nephew, Frank, who was three or four years old at the time, who actually found the present. Because he was always mesmerized with "'Granddad's big-truck,'" he always climbed the back bumper and up and over the tail gate when he could. That day after bending down to pick it up from the bed, he smiled as he showed it to me. After examining it closely, I noticed that it had my name on it. That present was found about a week after Christmas. John and Flora joked about that for days. I guess that was where they stashed the presents for Santa Claus. It makes sense now because all Santa'd have to do is drive in, park and pick up the bag of gifts from the back of the truck and walk inside with them. It was a good plan except for the fact that it was dark out there and if he dropped a gift in the back of the truck, it wouldn't be discovered until someone like Frank was playing in the bed.

But when we'd get the tree inside and decorated, we would stand back and wait for someone to plug in the lights for the tree. Man, that was a glorious sight. The icicles made the tree look as though it had twice as many lights as it actually did. Then, we'd spray the windows with the remaining snow—spraying close around the edges making it look like a frosty night even if it wasn't. So, after I'd get all excited about the tree and the family being there, I'd have to go to bed.

"Roger, it's almost time for Santa Claus and he won't come if you are up," my sister would say. Well, what kid would argue with that? So, to bed I'd go without a fight. In fact, I don't even recall having much trouble getting to sleep. One would think that it would be hard for an excited little boy to get to sleep when he was about to be visited by Santa, but somehow I'd get to sleep.

"Rog, he's been here; you better get up and see what he left you," Flora would say as she creaked open the bedroom door just enough for the darkness to receive a gleam of light. Unlike nowadays, I didn't seem to have any trouble waking up or even getting up. I'd jump up and walk into the front room where everyone would be looking at me to see my expression as I looked under the tree. Wow, those were special times.

Santa would always leave me a couple of toy

trucks and I remember playing with them inside until the weather got warm enough for me to take them outside to play in the dirt. Dirt, that was where these trucks belonged. So, in the summer that's where they got the most use.

Although all of the Christmases were special in Abydell, one Christmas really stands out in my mind. It was the year that when I woke up, Santa Claus was actually still there. He was standing right there in the front room ready to hand out my presents. But, there was a lot of commotion this particular year because my dog, Teddy, was growling and seemed ready to kill the man in the red suit. My whole family was trying to hold him back. Teddy wasn't normally a viscous little rat terrier, but this night he had turned into a different pet. In fact, because he normally wasn't a dog we ever worried about around guests, nobody expected him to become so fierce. He was barking his head off and nobody could actually catch him to calm him down or remove him from the room. And Santa didn't really expect Teddy to latch on to his leg like he did. He shook Santa's leg and Santa shook his own leg trying to get Teddy to let go. Needless to say, Mom and Dad were extremely embarrassed. I looked at the little dog hanging on for dear life as the red man shook his leg and when Mom finally got hold of the dog and made him loosen his teeth, I looked up I guess to see what Santa's facial expression was looking like. Whoa! One might say he was expelling a dark side of his disposition. --Not the cheerful white- faced Santa that I had seen before in town. This one didn't have red, pudgy cheeks either. This Santa's face was really brown. . .I mean he was really . . . a black Santa Claus. Needless to say, my dog was racist! Years later, I found out that one of my Dad's friends played Santa Claus for me that Christmas. His name was Bill, and all I really know is that he was a nice, black man from Paoli. I didn't expect to see a black Santa Claus because I had never seen one, since I grew up in a predominately white neighborhood. I guess Teddy had never seen one either.

To this very day, forty-some years later, nobody really knows what happened to Teddy. See, a few days after that night, he disappeared. Of course we missed the little black terrier, but we all figured that having a racial dog was wrong anyway.

13

Warts and Water

Growing up in Abydell left me with a great deal of appreciation for the simple life. That little village nestled just below the hill in the back and the railroad in the front is still my place to go when I recall the past. At forty-eight now, I still go to bed nearly every night praying that I may dream about it, experiencing the wonder of my childhood once again. In fact, to get to sleep sometimes, I still uncover my body so I can rekindle that chill that I once felt while living in that old house. However, in Abydell, in the winter I never had to fake being cold because it was real. Not as bad as Dad used to tell me it was when he was young growing up in Sandy Hook, but I knew cold. He often told about when he was young in his parent's home. According to Dad, it so airy that he would sometimes wake up on a bitter winter's morning finding traces of snow on his covers. Dad had apparently experienced a more harsh cold than I had.

Perhaps it was his past that kept our whole family content living in the old Abydell house. Dad was also one who knew what to do with warts when I burned the inside of my wrist when I had stumbled and braced myself on the front room stove. I burned my wrist on my left arm so badly that I carried a scab on the area for nearly three weeks. Then, after the area healed, I had developed some warts on my wrist. Can't explain it, but they appeared and couldn't get rid of them until I one day showed them to him for some reason or another. I think we were wrestling for fun, as we often did, and he grabbed my wrists and felt them there. Recalling that experience is funny because I can still feel his long, skinny fingers wrapped under my wrist and feeling that he felt something strange.

"What is this?" he asked.

"I don't know, but I've had them a long time."

"These are warts," he commented.

"Warts, what are warts?" I asked feeling that I may have some incurable disease.

"Oh they are common; have you been playing with a frog?"

"No, I don't touch frogs."

"Do you want to get rid of them?" he asked.

"I guess. . .what should I do?

"Well I can take them off and it won't hurt, but you have to promise that you will not ask me how I do it and you won't look at the area for a whole week." He said this seriously. One could always tell when he was joking because a twinkle appeared in his eyes. Then he'd reach to adjust his ball cap. He'd lift it up off his head and lightly set it back in his head so the bill leaned forward and the back sat on top higher than normal. None of that happened that time. He wasn't kidding. But, of course I had to ask him why I couldn't look at the warts for a whole week.

"I can't tell you how it works or it won't

work—the warts won't go away."

"Okay, I guess." I commented. And at that point he left the room and returned with a little, white tissue; I believe it was a cigarette rolling paper or something like that. After asking me to hold out my bare wrist, he told me to close my eyes and not look at what he was doing. I did as he asked and I can still feel what he did. It was painless. It tickled a little as he made a slow X on the area—I believe it was an X from one wart to the other. Then, he covered it up with some gauze.

"Now don't look at it for a week."

I didn't think I could resist looking for a whole week, but I managed. Needless to say, when I looked the warts were gone and have not returned to this day. I still have no idea how he did it. The secret died with him in 1985. Likewise, he could also find water with a willow branch and I saw him do it. The branch pointed straight down where he found water and he showed me the bark still in his hands where he had tried to hold the branch so it wouldn't turn in his hands. Although this was a great trick to me, the warts trick was one that cannot be explained by anyone I have ever told the story to.

14

My Cousins

Since my grandparents lived a short distance from us in a small section of West Baden called Russelville, they were often visited by my aunts and uncles from the Muncie and Newcastle Indiana areas. However, on my mom's side of the family, I only knew a cousin named Earl who lived with his parents, Uncle Ross and Aunt Laura (Laurie as Mom called her.) Laura was very close to Mom and they spent a great deal of time together until she acquired cancer in about 1971. Uncle Ross Barton was a highly favored uncle and I miss him often. He called Dad "Harry-Blueberry," and of course I was "Little Harry." He had been a wrestler before when he lived in Ohio, Dad told me. He and Dad worked for the Indiana State Highway Department. Uncle Ross was somewhat of a jokester. He specifically enjoyed showing the strength in his hands by grasping Dad's thigh (close to his knee) and squeezing until Dad begged for mercy. My uncle was so strong that according to Dad, once he saw Ross twist a cow's ear so hard with only one hand that the cow dropped to its knees! They shared a salt truck during the winter months and mowed along Highway 56 in the hot Southern Indiana summers. Dad often flagged while others worked their various jobs. Other times he would swing a mowing scythe to cut grass where mowing machines couldn't reach. Even though it was a tough job, I got the impression that he truly loved his job. Unfortunately for him, it was only available to him when the Democrats were in office. So, since my parents were both close to the Bartons, I got to know Earl pretty well. Earl was Ross and Laura's only son; Laura had been married once before to Barber Atkins, who died and was buried back in Sandy Hook, Kentucky. I didn't know him, but did meet Homer, a son, a few times. Homer lived in Ohio and drove a semi, if I recall correctly, and also ran his own gas station there. There was a couple other brothers I believe named Leonard Atkins and Junior Atkins. Junior, I was told, died as young boy early after acquiring Leukemia. But, Earl Barton was more my age—probably about five years older. He loved to have family over and was always up to something. Specifically, he enjoyed working on automobiles back when I was young. Our families would for one reason or another ride back into the hills on their tractor to a beautiful tract of land where I believe Ross and Laura once lived. When we visited I got to ride along side Uncle Ross on the tractor while others would be pulled along on the hay wagon. He would drive the old, green tractor back the muddy, washed out road to the open field where an old, rickety house still remained. The house was where Uncle Ross and Aunt Laura once lived when they first moved to Indiana. We would walk around the field looking for seedlings and wild black berries. Mom and Dad would reset the pines back at Abydell. Mom loved pine trees, although she said none of them ever grew for her. This is hard to believe because she could usually make anything grow. Later, after Laura had passed away, I recall visiting Uncle Ross as he worked firing the boiler for I guess was the Cornwell Company. I suppose it was the Cornwell Company because that is where the boiler was located. The Cornwells owned a cabinet factory in Paoli for many years until a fire destroyed it sometime in the late sixties.

As for the cousins from the Elliott side of the family, my Aunt Isabelle Sanders had a daughter, who was closer to Flora's age—I don't recall much about her when I was young, however she has told me that when I was a baby, she loved to sleep with me when she spent the night with Flora. My Uncle Jack lived in Louisville, Kentucky and I would say was the "backbone" of the family. Unfortunately, he died when I was in high school of lung cancer. His daughters were Debbie, Dana, and he had a son named David. I have fond recollections of Debbie and Dana, but cannot recall much of anything we ever did together. David, on the other hand, was a different story. On the first occasion that I recall David spending a few days at Abydell, I experienced a troubling situation. He and I were playing in the front yard near the gravel driveway when a friend who lived down under the hill, came to visit me. The friend's name was Danny Baker and the Bakers and the Elliotts had been long time friends spending time together on weekends playing ball, pitching horse shoes and attending each other's birthday parties. The Bakers were very instrumental to my parents back then because they had a car and we didn't have one until I was about four. For some reason Danny and David were not able to get along from the very start. In fact, it was only a few minutes before found them locked up in a fight where I recall David getting in a few precise punches to Danny's chin. For some reason those blows made me take Danny's side. I was mixed up on why it upset me so to see them fight and I couldn't understand why I felt sorry for Danny. Maybe it was that I knew him better or it may have been that David actually initiated the fight. To this day, I still cannot recall why they didn't like each other and it took only a few minutes before they began to throw punches. I don't even know why they were fighting! Danny was a good friend. David was always a good cousin.

Each time he came to our house he was always welcomed by my parents. As a matter of fact, he was the only cousin on Dad's side that didn't get on Dad's nerves. For some reason Dad was impatient with my Aunt Faye Warren's boys, probably because they often ran on their own a great deal and Dad did not approve of this at all. They were always good to me, but to Dad they seemed to need some guidance. The last time as kids I spent some time with Terry Warren was when he stayed few days with me at Abydell. There, he and I crossed over the fence in the back yard and cut branches from the huge river birch trees to make a hut. It was Terry's idea; I suppose he learned this trait from watching Tarzan on TV. Building the hut was a lot of fun for us, however Dad didn't like the fact that the hut eventually dammed up the branch and caused him some hard work to clear it out. We never really had any bad times together, but I do recall that he wasn't very happy with me one time. It was after I was visiting him at his home in Russelville. On this occasion I told on him for smoking ciga-rettes in the basement of the house. But for the most part, he was a few years older than me and I always looked up to him. He seemed to be a popular kid in school, especially with the girls. A few years back, Terry and I were talking about how Dad was tough on him. He specifically recalled that one summer Dad tried to make him a baseball catcher. Dad told me that he was pretty good too. But, Terry only remembered that Uncle Hollie taught him to catch and he was very strict in his teaching. I bet that if Terry would have kept playing baseball after that, Dad would have followed him to every game he played. Terry also had a couple of brothers, Zane and Jerry. They were older than him. They were called cousins, but I didn't really get to know them. There was an older brother too, named Wayne. I don't recall anything about him except he spent most of his time with his dad, Elwood, in Morehead, Kentucky.

Mammaw Menta's birthdays were a time when all of my aunts and uncles came to West Baden. We would all gather at Kimball's shelter house and eventually eat ice cream and cake and get to know each other. Aunt Lucy and Uncle Woody would bring Elaine, Diane and Linda from Muncie. Aunt Jewell would come bringing Sherry and Ginger from New Castle. She also had a son named Myron, but he nor Uncle Russ ever attended the reunions to my recollection. Aunt Jewell also had another son named Alvin Carl, who had been killed in a motorcycle accident in New Castle so I didn't get to know him. Aunt Roxie brought Steve and Marshall when I was young. Aunt Isabelle brought her only daughter, Mary Alice. Mary Alice was married by this time to Johnny Spurgeon, a golfing enthusiast, in French Lick. If you recall, she used to spend time with my sister, Flora, and she always liked to sleep with me when I was just a baby. Uncle Jack would bring Debbie, Dana, and David from Louisville. Everyone would bring a dish and it was a wonderful time. Everyone was so nice and proud of their respective families and unlike many of us today, never forgot about the true meaning of family.

15

Harvey Franklin Elliott

If there was anyone who deserved to have his own chapter in this book, it is Harvey. So understood, yet misunderstood. To begin, Harvey was my only living brother. He was loved by all, but understood by few. I'm not sure I can preserve his life here, but I'd like to pay him homage. From what I can tell, he was once very normal. In fact, I've read some of his earlier writing and found him to have once been a very gifted writer. When I was born, Harvey was in the Army, stationed in Korea. I'll have to say that I did not know him all that well because when he returned, he wasn't the same as when he left to enlist. Recently, a man who lived close to him in West Baden told me that people around there always felt that he was acting crazy to get his military pension. But, believe me he wasn't acting. He was emotionally distraught for many years. He heard voices almost constantly. He felt people were out to get him. He was in constant anguish for not being allowed to see his beloved children, Frank and Terri. Their mother divorced Harvey when they were young and eventually moved them to Florida where he couldn't be with them at all. After a few years of living alone, Harvey remarried Jeannetta Moore, from Shoals, in the late sixties and remained with her until his death this year. Both Harvey and Jeanetta were confined to a nursing home when he acquired Leukemia and passed away in Florida while being cared for by his daughter Terri and son Frank. Although Harvey loved fishing, he was constantly bothered by Schizophrenia until he finally had to spend his time inside where he felt safe. He apparently had allowed himself and Jeanetta to drink too much over this time and finally both of them became Schizophrenic. They both became so pitiful and also so difficult to be around that when I'd attempt to visit, Harvey would get nervous, talk to those voices he would hear, and eventually pick a fight with me. This went on for about 30 years. People who did not visit him had no idea what was going on. Apparently, they thought he was just a recluse and wanted to keep from working so as to keep getting a check from the Army. After many years, I too, often wondered what had caused him to change so drastically after his time in the Army. So, it was my understanding that while Harvey was in Korea, although it was not considered war time, he had been missing for a time. He had apparently been a prisoner of the North Koreans and had to be given a series of electrical shocks while he was in the hospital in order to forget what he had seen or encountered. All I know is that he was the company's field operator and that he once told me "'For the most part over there it was peaceful, but there were times when the North Koreans would break through the lines and we would have to drive them back.'" I got the idea that this was an all-out war until they got the job done. But, he could not recall anything else. He must have experienced an enormous amount of pain for our Army doctors to decide to give him cerebral shock treatments so he couldn't remember what happened. Well, he didn't remember specifics, but he was always a nervous misfit afterwards. He didn't trust anyone and I'm sure that is why his first marriage couldn't work. He also didn't trust his second wife and this caused them problems too. He wouldn't go anywhere very long without her being with him. I'm nearly positive that this is why she remained intoxicated most of the time. I do know he loved his family and my mom and dad were constantly having to care for him throughout their lives.

16

Harve Burns Elliott

An old expression that my family brought back with them from the hills of Kentucky portrayed a tough, older person who was hard to keep down even when times were extremely tough. This expression apparently was instilled in my grandfather, Harve Burns Elliott. As I remember him, he must have been the personification of it. So, the expression "tough ole bird" fit my grandfather for several reasons. This was apparent since my Uncle Jack had been named for my granddad. My brother, Harvey had also been named for my Granddad Harve. Uncle Jack Elliott probably went by his middle because they were both at home at the same time. That just made sense, especially at supper or when Mammaw was calling someone for something. Otherwise it would have been too confusing. As mentioned in chapter two, Harve died in 1981; but the description given then was of a feeble old man. However, earlier in his life he was anything but feeble. The childish, old man who moved to New Castle, Indiana later in his life so his daughters could watch over him, was the same man who once killed poisonous snakes by picking them up by the tails and cracking them like a whip! The old man who would cry when we had to leave him after a short visit was the same one who moved from Sandy Hook to Russelville, Indiana and took care of his own "doctoring." To be more specific, because we lived within five miles of my grandparents when I was young, Dad used to often call "over home" to see how his parents were. I don't really know why Dad referred to their place as "over home," but he did. He also never called them Mom and Dad; instead he called them "Mammy and Poppie." Anyway, one day as Dad called to check on "Poppie" because he knew he had been having a tooth ache, "Mammy" answered the phone and told Dad that Granddad couldn't talk on the phone because he was out on the back porch. Actually, she implied that Granddad was not to be disturbed because he was out there pulling the tooth. Well, Dad understood and decided to leave him alone. So, after about an hour, Dad called again to see if Granddad was feeling any better. Again, Mammaw answered the phone. This time she commented that he's still outside. Well, Dad told Mom we were going "over home." She and I got into the old pick up and the three of us started out. When we got there he seemed to be doing better. He was sitting on the front porch. This was where he often was when we arrived so we expected that he was better. As we walked down the steps from the street, he sat still. He was very pale and he was biting on a white cloth. He couldn't talk. He was still in pain. So, Mom asked him if he maybe should go on to the dentist, he shook his head and appeared angered. At that point everone seemed to chime in and insist that Granddad get to the doctor. What we didn't know at the time was that this "tough ole bird" had taken care of the situation himself by pulling not one but all of his teeth with a pair of pliers! Not believing in going to a medical doctor and never having been to a dentist (as far as I knew), he had developed an incredible pain tolerance.

With this kind of pain tolerance, I still cannot understand how this old mountain man who came from Eastern Kentucky, was ever squirmish about anything that life had to offer. However, there was one thing he just couldn't shake. See, according to Dad, Granddad was once an accomplished five-string banjo player, but I had never heard him play. I hadn't even seen a musical instrument "over home." Over the years I had heard numerous times that he was once a very good musician. But there was somehow an unwritten rule about never mentioning the banjo around "Poppie." With this on my mind one day, and because I felt I could ask Granddad anything, I figured on asking him about the days when he played. I just wanted to hear him play, after all I really didn't know what a banjo sounded like first hand. So, while Granddad was sitting in his chair near the front door I proceded to inquire about it.

"Granddad, can you still play the banjo?"

"What? How do you know?"

"I just heard you were good."

"Yeh, I use to."

"Do you ever play anymore?"

"New, I don't. Haven't played since I was back in Sandy Hook."

"Could you play if you really wanted too— if you got your fingers back in shape?"

"Don't know, but will never know. I won't play that thing anymore. Something happened. I can't play again."

I knew by the tone of his voice that he didn't want to be questioned about it any more. So, I waited until I could ask Dad about why Granddad didn't play music anymore. Although he looked at me closely before he rendered an answer, he finally told me that Granddad told him that back in Kentucky, Granddad was sitting playing his banjo when something happened. He said that is why he wouldn't play any longer.

"Yeh, that's what Granddad said. But, what happened?" I asked.

"Well he said he was just sittin' there playin' like he always did...In his chair, but he was playin' his banjo a fast one. And right in the middle of the playin' he heard something right above his head. It was somethin' in the attic. It sounded like it was dancin' along with the music. Well, he said it scared him so much that he put it down and never picked it up again."

"What was it?" I asked again.

"Don't know. All I know is that he never played again and told me after that happen'd he felt it was wrong to play—like it was sacreligous. --He had it in his mind that the devil or somthin' was in the attic when he was playin' and figured that if that was happenin', it must be wrong to play."

This was, remember, the same man who was tough enough to kill snakes with his bare hands and yank out every tooth in his mouth with a pair of pliers! But sure enough, something happened that day in Kentucky that scared him nearly senseless.

But on the other side of the family tree my other grandfather, John Skaggs, my mother's father, played a musical instrument up until the last few years of his life. He lived 98 years and even though he continued to play the fiddle, he apparently was never visited by the dancing evil that apparently tapped the life out of Granddad Elliott's banjo playing.

17

Us, Today

All of us came from this same stock. Our elders were tough, tight-knitted and weren't afraid of change. But, my generation really doesn't know much about each other. In fact, we are so spread out that we don't even recognize each other without someone to point us out to each other. Our new family motto is something like this: "I love you and I'll see you at your funeral (if I can get off work)." However, Dad frequently told me of an old saying they had back in the hills of Kentucky: "'Give me my flowers when I'm alive.'" Likewise, he also said, "'I hope when I'm dead and gone that you don't forget where the graveyard is.'" He also added this one when anyone in the family was arguing: "'Be careful what you say to each other because one day one of you'll be looking down in the casket at the other one's pale face and you may feel sorry you said what you said.'" I'm sure that this advice may have come from experience. Remember, he was the oldest of thirteen and several of his siblings had died before him. Five of them died as mere children and one as a teenager.

Even after moving away from their Kentucky roots, Dad and Mom still kept in touch with the people down there. They'd even drive back to Sandy Hook to visit grave sites on decoration day. Unfortunately though, he had to stop when he became so "worn out" he couldn't easily make the trip. Also, Dad always believed that people should care for the sanctity of a grave site. I learned this while he was the caretaker of the city graveyard in Paoli, Indiana. While he and I were there I was taught to never walk direcly on the graves because he felt it was disrespectful to the dead. But, today, when we meet at the funeral homes to pay our last respects to our beloved Aunts and Uncles, we are merely strangers in an age where there are more modes of communication than ever before. We all have letters that should be written, cards that should be mailed, calls that should be initiated and even emails and text messages that are waiting to be sent.

Why just last summer I met some cousins on my mother's side that I have never met, or at least to my recollection. And if it had not been for my sister, who recalled that these people exist in the Morehead area, I would never have even known they were close relatives. Needless to say, I truly enjoyed finding and meeting these people and hearing their stories. Stories that would have been dead possibly, if somebody like me hadn't stirred up the conversations.

They shared where my parents once lived before I was born. And hearing them tell me about what happened when they visited this place and that one brought about a welcomed peace. The more they told me, the more I wanted to know as we drove the hills of Kentucky. This was a peace that only family can experience together.

Moreover, after visiting Kentucky and parts of Indiana in the past years, I have allowed my own children, who of course are growing up way too fast, to at least get to know many of my distant-cousins. I hope my kids some day will also get the urge to find out more since they now know of the places where their grandparents once lived and where my grandparents lived, struggled and moved from because of hard times associated with the depression. When their interests mature, and it seems to happen to many of us awfully late in life, I hope my daughters will share some stories I've passed on.

Closing

If you have been mentioned in this book, you or your story has somehow inspired me. And if I don't have a delightful story to share at this point that pertains to you, I hope that we will not continue to be strangers. For I hope anyone can see, that I relish the stories from my long-lost family members, my closest friends, and my own past. So, with this I encourage my current family and friends to spend time together telling and retelling stories that can be relayed to future generations. And instead of waiting until someone dies to pay your respects, I urge you to get out and rekindle the past with them while they are still alive. I also urge the reader to spend time with aging loved-ones. Not only do they need your support, but you may also find they still can recall some very intriguing stories. —Stories that most definitely will die with them if we do not take the time to ask about what "back then" was like.

We cannot keep people alive forever. But as long as their stories are being retold, the spirit in which we retell their stories keeps the people themselves always with us.

LaVergne, TN USA
16 June 2010
186414LV00001B/52/P

9 781432 750121